Fourth edition

New
Headway

Beginner Workbook with key

John and Liz Soars

OXFORD
UNIVERSITY PRESS

Contents

Go to **elt.oup.com/student/headway** to access the audio.

1

Introductions • *am/are/is* • What's this in English?
• Numbers 1–10 • Plurals • Good morning!

Hello!

Introductions

1 🎧 Complete the conversations.

My	I'm	name's

1 **A** Hello. ___I'm___ Adam.

2 **B** Hello. _____ name's Bonnie.

3 **C** Hello. My_____ Chris.

2 🎧 Complete the conversations.

your	My (x2)	name	What's

1 **A** I'm Alex. ___What's___ your name?
  B Belle.

2 **B** _____ name's Kate.
  What's _____ name?
  C Charlie.

3 **H** I'm Harry. What's your _____?
  A _____ name's Alfie.

am/are/is

Nice to meet you

3 🎧 Complete the conversations.

1 **A** Carl, this is Liliana Moretti.
   C Hello, Liliana. My name's Carl Erikson.
   L Hello, Carl. Nice _____ _____ you.

2 **B** Ruby, _____ _____ Husain Malouf.
   R Hello, Husain. _____ _____ meet you.
   H _____ you.

3 **C** Liliana, _____ _____ Ruby. Ruby, _____ _____ Liliana.
   L Hello, Ruby. _____ Liliana Moretti.
   R Hello. _____ Ruby Harrison.
   L _____ _____ _____ you.
   R And _____ .

4 Are these first names or surnames?

~~Smith~~	~~John~~	Ella	McKenna	Luke
Robert	Bond	Ruby	Johnson	Alice
Harry	Sophie	Joshua	Blackman	Catherine

First names	John
Surnames	Smith

How are you?

5 🎧 Put the words in order to make conversations.

1   are / you / How
   E Hi, Ben. _How_ _are_ _you_ ?

   thanks / Fine
   B _____ _____ , Ella. And you?

   OK / I'm / thank
   E _____ _____ _____ you.

2   you / How / are
   C Hello, Michael. _____ _____ _____?

   well / very / you / And
   M I'm _____ _____ , thanks. _____ _____?

3   Alice / Hi
   R _____ _____. How are you?

   How / you / are
   A I'm fine, thank you, Robert. _____ _____ _____?

   thank / well / Very
   R _____ _____ _____ you.

Vocabulary

What's this in English?

6 Look at the pictures and complete the crossword.

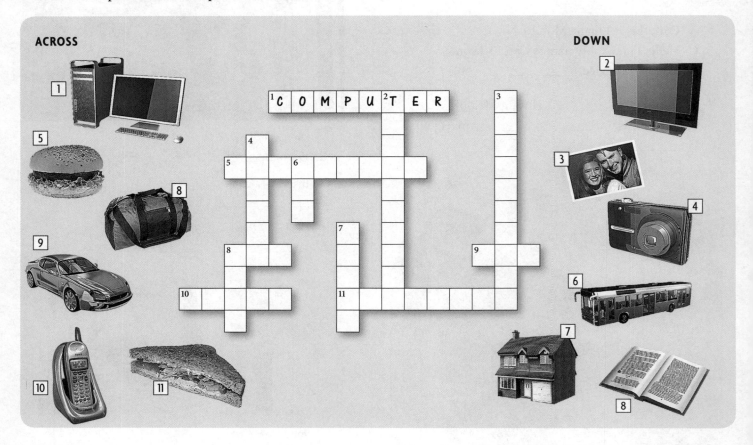

ACROSS

DOWN

Across clue 1: C O M P U T E R

Numbers 1–10

7 Write the numbers in full.

two   seven   _____   _____   _____

_____   _____   _____   _____   _____

8 🎧 Write the numbers you hear.

<u> 4 </u>   <u> 8 </u>   <u>   </u>   <u>   </u>   <u>   </u>   <u>   </u>   <u>   </u>

Plurals

9 Write what you see in the pictures.

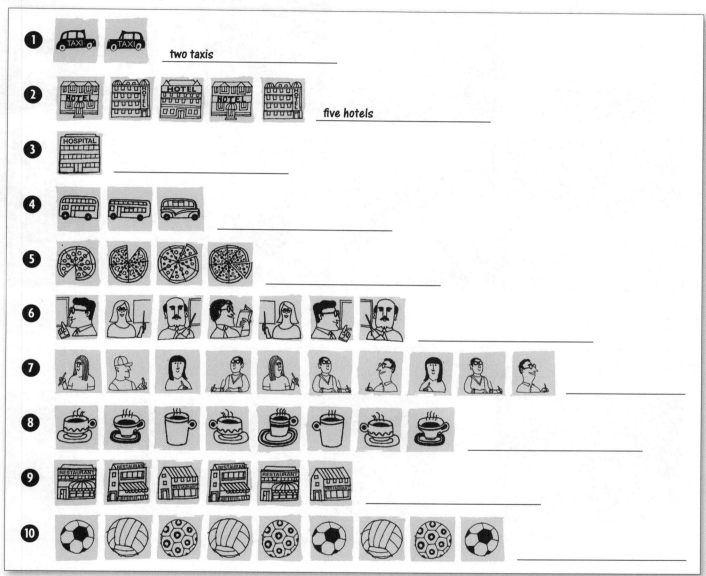

1. two taxis
2. five hotels
3. _____
4. _____
5. _____
6. _____
7. _____
8. _____
9. _____
10. _____

10 🎧 Listen and write the words in the chart.

restaurants	hotels
buses	footballs
taxis	hospitals
sandwiches	coffees
houses	pizzas
teachers	students
photographs	

/s/	/z/	/ɪz/
restaurants	hotels	buses

Listen and repeat.

Everyday English

Good morning!

11 🎧 Write the conversations.

| Goodbye! | ~~Good morning!~~ | Goodnight! | Good afternoon! |

12 🎧 Complete the conversations.

| A cup of tea, please. | ~~What a lovely day today!~~ | Bye! See you tomorrow! |
| Have a nice day! | Sleep well! | Bye! See you later! |

1 **A** What a lovely day today!
  B It is, isn't it?

2 **A** _____
  B Yes. After school.

3 **A** _____
  B And you.

4 **A** _____
  B Certainly.

5 **A** _____
  B Bye!

6 **A** _____
  B Goodnight!

Don't forget!

Grammar

13 Complete the chart.

Verb *to be*		Short form
I	*am*	
You		*You're*
It		

14 Complete the sentences with words in the box.

'm	are	's

1 I **'m** James.
2 What _____ your name?
3 How _____ you?
4 My name _____ Katherine.
5 I _____ fine, thanks.
6 _____ you OK?
7 It _____ a book.

15 Write the correct answer.

1 **My** name's Pablo.
  a **I**   b **My**

2 How are _____?
  a **you**   b **your**

3 What _____ your name?
  a **'s**   b **are**

4 _____'m very well.
  a **I**   b **My**

5 I'm fine, thank _____.
  a **you**   b **your**

6 What's _____ name?
  a **you**   b **your**

16 <u>Underline</u> the correct answer.

1 **A** Hello, Alice!
  B I'm very well. / <u>Hi, John!</u>

2 **A** How are you, Alice?
  B I'm fine, thanks. / Nice to meet you.

3 **A** Nice to meet you.
  B I'm fine. / And you.

4 **A** Goodbye!
  B Bye! See you tomorrow! / Thank you.

5 **A** What's this in English?
  B Is book. / It's a book.

Punctuation

17 Write capital letters where they are necessary.

1 i'm peter. what's your name?
  I'm Peter. What's your name?

2 my name's anna.
  _____

3 what's this in english?
  _____

4 it's a computer.
  _____

5 how are you, mika?
  _____

6 i'm fine, thank you.
  _____

am **is** my

are

your

2

Countries • *am/are/is* • *Her name's. . . /She's from. . .*
• Questions • Adjectives *good/awful. . .* • Numbers 11–30

Countries

1 Look at the pictures and complete the crossword.

⁴H U N G A R Y

ACROSS

4   7

8   9

10   12

DOWN

1   2

3   5   6   11

2   Write the countries from the crossword in the correct column.

●	●●	●●	●●●	●●●●	●●●●
Spain	China	Japan			

Listen and repeat.

am/are/is

Her name's. . . /She's from. . .

3 Write the words in the correct column.

she	~~James~~	Anna	his
Tatiana	her	Henry	he

♀	she
♂	James

4 Complete the sentences with the words *His* or *Her*.

a __Her__ name's Rosely.
b _____ name's László.
c _____ name's Yong.
d _____ name's Tatiana.

5 Complete the sentences with the words *She's* or *He's*.

a __He's__ Simon.
b _____ Hayley.
c _____ Kevin.
d _____ Karima.

6 Complete the sentences with words from the box.

She's	He's	Her	His

1 __His__ name's Yong. __He's__ from China.
2 _____ name's Hayley. _____ from Australia.
3 _____ name's Karima. _____ from Egypt.
4 _____ name's Kevin. _____ from the United States.
5 _____ name's Rosely. _____ from Brazil.
6 _____ name's Simon. _____ from England.
7 _____ name's Tatiana. _____ from Russia.
8 _____ name's László. _____ from Hungary.

7 🎧 Listen and match a question in **A** with an answer in **B**.

A	B
1 What's her name?	☐ a His name's David.
2 Where's she from?	☐1 b Her name's Carla.
3 What's his name?	☐ c He's from England.
4 Where's he from?	☐ d She's from Italy.

Listening

At a party

8 🎧 Listen and complete the conversation.

J Hello! What's your name?

S __My_____ name's Svana.

J Hi, Svana. _____ Jeff.

S _____, Jeff.

J _____ are you, Svana?

S I'm _____, thanks.

J Where _____ from, Svana?

S _____ Oslo.

J Oh! Is that in Sweden?

S No! _____ in Norway, of course!

J Oh, yes! Look at that girl! Over there!

S Yes, _____ name's Ingrid.

J _____ from?

S She _____ from Norway too.

J Is she a friend?

S _____ my sister.

J Oh!

Questions

9 🎧 Match a question in **A** and an answer in **B**.

A	B
1 What's his name?	☐ a I'm fine, thank you.
2 Where's she from?	☐1 b His name's Henry.
3 How are you?	☐ c It's a dictionary.
4 Are you from Italy?	☐ d It's in London.
5 What's this in English?	☐ e She's from Japan.
6 Where's Buckingham Palace?	☐ f Yes, I am. I'm from Milan.

Adjectives

good/awful

10 Write an adjective on the correct line.

good	awful	fantastic
~~really good~~	OK	~~bad~~

🙂 _____

🙂🙂 *really good*

🙂🙂🙂 _____

😐 _____

🙁 *bad*

🙁🙁 _____

Reading

11 🎧 Read about the people. Where are they? Write in a country – Egypt, Malaysia or England.

Where are they?

Ann and James are on holiday. They're in Europe. The weather is bad, but the holiday is really good. The food is OK.

The building in the photograph is over 150 years old. It is the home of kings and queens. It's in the centre of the city.

'It's a fantastic building,' says Ann.

They're in _____

Carla and Pedro are on holiday. They're in Africa. The weather is very good, and the holiday is great. 'The people are really nice,' says Carla, 'but the heat is awful.'

The buildings in the photograph are in a desert near a town.

They are 5,000 years old. They are the homes of dead kings and queens.

They're in _____

Catherine and Anthony are on holiday. They're in Asia.

The weather is OK, and the holiday is really good.

The food is international.

The buildings in the photograph are in a park. They're new just 12 years old. They are offices for petrol companies and other businesses.

'The buildings are beautiful,' says Anthony.

They're in _____

12 Are the sentences true (✓) or false (✗)?

Ann and James

1 ✓ They are on holiday.
2 ☐ They are in the United States.
3 ☐ The building is old.

Carla and Pedro

4 ☐ They are in England.
5 ☐ The holiday is really good.
6 ☐ The building is very old.

Catherine and Anthony

7 ☐ They are in Europe.
8 ☐ The holiday is awful.
9 ☐ The buildings are new.

Listening

She's from Berlin

Sofia

13 🎧 Listen to Sofia and Adam.
<u>Underline</u> the correct answer.

1 She's from <u>*Berlin*</u> / *Birmingham*.
2 Sofia is *a doctor* / *a teacher*.
3 Her *school* / *hospital* is in the centre of town.
4 Her students are from *Germany* / *the US*.

5 Adam is from *Los Angeles* / *Sydney*.
6 He's *a doctor* / *a teacher*.
7 His *school* / *hospital* is in the centre of town.
8 The building is *awful* / *fantastic*.

14 🎧 <u>Underline</u> what you hear.

1 *He's* / <u>*She's*</u> a teacher.
2 *She's* / *He's* a doctor.
3 *Her* / *His* name's Adam.
4 *His* / *Her* name's Sofia.
5 *She's* / *He's* married.
6 *He's* / *She's* married.
7 *Her* / *His* students are from the US.
8 *His* / *He's* from Sydney

Adam

Everyday English

Numbers 11–30

15 Match the numbers and the words.

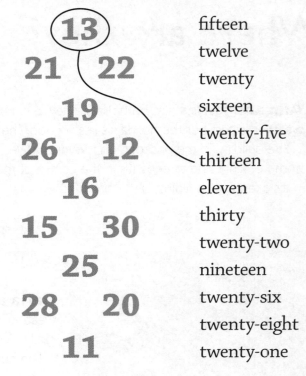

13   21   22   19   26   12   16   15   30   25   28   20   11

fifteen
twelve
twenty
sixteen
twenty-five
thirteen
eleven
thirty
twenty-two
nineteen
twenty-six
twenty-eight
twenty-one

16 Write the numbers.

23	twenty-three	17	seventeen
11	_____	29	_____
18	_____	24	_____
14	_____	27	_____

17 🎧 Listen. Write the numbers you hear.

15   28   ____   ____

____   ____   ____

Don't forget!

Grammar

18 Complete the chart.

Verb *to be*		Short form
I		*I'm*
You		
He		*He's*
She	*is*	
It		
They		

19 Complete the sentences with a word in the box.

'm	are	's	is	're

1 How __are__ you today?
  I _____ very well, thanks.

2 Where _____ you from, Suzanne?
  I _____ from France.

3 Where _____ Jack and Maria on holiday?
  They _____ in Florida.

4 _____ the weather good?
  Yes, it _____. It _____ fantastic.

5 Where _____ they from?
  Maria _____ from Spain. Jack _____ from Canada.

20 Write the correct answer.

1 **A** Where's Maria from?
  B __She's__ from Spain.
    a **He's**   b **She's**

2 **A** Is that man from Germany?
  B No, _____ from Italy.
    a **his**   b **he's**

3 **A** Is he a student?
  B Yes. _____ is Freddy.
    a **His name**   b **He's name**

4 **A** How are you today?
  B _____
    a **Fine, thanks. And you?**   b **Thank you. OK?**

5 **A** Goodbye! Have a nice day!
  B _____
    a **Very well.**   b **Thank you. And you.**

Vocabulary

21 Write the word in English.

1 __a computer__   5 _____
2 _____   6 _____
3 _____   7 _____
4 _____   8 _____

Pronunciation

22 *Your* and *you're* are pronounced the same /jɔ:/.
Complete the sentences with *your* or *you're*.

1 What's __your__ name?
2 __You're__ from Japan.
3 _____ a student.
4 This is _____ book.
5 _____ from Moscow.
6 Is this _____ phone?

🎧 Listen and repeat.

he's

his   her

she's

3

Jobs • *am / are / is* • Questions and negatives
• Vocabulary revision • Social expressions (1)

Jobs

1 Look at the pictures and complete the crossword.

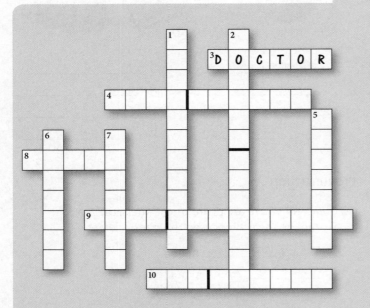

ACROSS

DOWN

³D O C T O R

is or *isn't*?

2 Complete the sentences.

1 He __isn't__ a bus driver.
   He _____ a taxi driver.

2 She _____ a police officer.
   She _____ a shop assistant.

3 It _____ a phone.
   It _____ a camera.

Questions and negatives

is/isn't

3 Complete the identity card.

ADDRESS
~~SURNAME~~
PHONE NUMBER
JOB
FIRST NAME
MOBILE NUMBER
AGE
MARRIED
~~SIGNATURE~~
COUNTRY

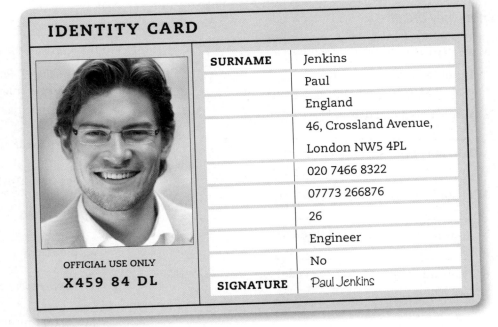

IDENTITY CARD

OFFICIAL USE ONLY
X459 84 DL

SURNAME	Jenkins
	Paul
	England
	46, Crossland Avenue, London NW5 4PL
	020 7466 8322
	07773 266876
	26
	Engineer
	No
SIGNATURE	*Paul Jenkins*

4 🎧 Write the questions about Paul in exercise 3.

1 __What's his surname?__
   Jenkins.

2 _____ ?
   Paul.

3 _____ ?
   England.

4 _____ ?
   46, Crossland Avenue, London NW5 4PL.

5 _____ ?
   020 7466 8322.

6 _____ ?
   07773 266876.

7 _____ ?
   26.

8 _____ ?
   He's an engineer.

9 _____ ?
   No, he isn't.

5 🎧 Correct the information about Paul.

1 His surname is Ford.
   __His surname isn't Ford. It's Jenkins.__

2 He's from Australia.
   _____

3 He's 23.
   _____

4 He's a student.
   _____

5 He's married.
   _____. He's single.

6 🎧 Answer the questions about Paul. Use short answers.

1 Is his surname Jenkins?
   __Yes, it is.__

2 Is he from Canada?
   __No, he isn't.__

3 Is he from London?
   _____

4 Is he 24?
   _____

5 Is he a student?
   _____

6 Is he an engineer?
   _____

Negatives and questions

I'm not/they aren't

7 Make negative and positive sentences.

1 I / not / a teacher. I / student
I'm not a teacher. I'm a student.

2 Peter / not / a taxi driver. He / a bus driver.

_____

3 We / not / from Spain. We / from Italy.

_____

4 I / not married. I / single.

_____

5 You / not / a nurse. You / a student.

_____

6 Paul and Donny McNab / not / doctors. They / singers in a band.

_____

8 Look at the photo of the band, _Metro 5_.
Write the correct answer.

1 Paul and Donny __are__ brothers.
a **is**   b **are**

2 They _____ from Scotland. They're from Ireland.
a **aren't**   b **isn't**

3 **A** Who are the singers in your band?
B We _____ all singers!
a **am**   b **are**

4 **A** Are you a bus driver?
B _____ a bus driver! I'm a builder!
a **I no**   b **I'm not**

5 **A** Are you tired at the moment?
B We _____ tired! We're very happy!
a **aren't**   b **isn't**

6 Bo _____ married. Ronan is married.
a **is no**   b **isn't**

9 Put the words in the correct order to make questions.

1 from / brothers / Where / the / are
Where are the brothers from _____?
They're from Ireland.

2 from / Bo / Sweden / Is
_____?
No, he's from Australia.

3 his / job / What's
_____?
He's a nurse.

4 on / Where / tour / are / they
_____?
They're on tour in the United States.

5 Lisa / band / Is / with / the
_____?
No, she isn't. She's in Australia.

METRO 5

Listening

An interview with Ella

10 🎧 Listen to the conversation with Ella. Complete the information.

IDENTITY CARD		OFFICIAL USE ONLY X28997DL

First name	Ella
Surname	
Age	
Address	209 Park Place
	NY 11217
Work number	212-786-
Cell phone	917-438-
Job	
Married	
Signature	*Ella Smith*

11 Complete the lines from the interview.

1 I know your __first__ name's Ella, but what's your __surname__ ?

2 How _____ are you, Ella?

3 And you live in Brooklyn, right? What's your _____ ?

4 What's your _____ number at _____ ?

5 What's your _____ phone number?

6 Now, you work in newspapers, but what's _____ _____ ?

7 And, _____ _____ married?

Vocabulary

Revision

12 Complete the words from this unit.

1 It's a lovely day. I'm very h a p p y .

2 My book is good. It's very i _ _ _ r _ _ t _ n g .

3 *Metro 5* is a b _ n _ . All five of them are s _ _ g _ r _ .

4 New York is a c _ t _ . The t _ w _ where I live is very small.

5 Mike is at work. He's very t _ r _ _ .

6 My brother Tony is very d _ _ f _ _ _ _ n t from me. We aren't the same.

7 The train s _ _ _ t _ _ _ n is in the centre of town.

8 **A** Where are you?
   B I'm h _ r _ ! Where are you?

9 **A** どこの駅ですか？
   B I'm sorry. I don't u _ _ _ _ _ s t _ _ _ d .

10 Suzie is very e _ c _ _ e _ _ . It's her birthday tomorrow.

Everyday English

Social expressions (1)

13 🎧 Write a line from the box in the correct place.

| I'm sorry. | A cup of tea, please. | Excuse me! | That's all right. | I don't understand. | I don't know. |

1 **A** A cup of tea, please.
  B That's 90p.

2 **A** _____
  B Don't worry. It's OK.

3 **A** Thank you very much.
  B _____

4 **A** _____! Can I have the menu, please?
  B Certainly.

5 **A** どこの駅ですか?
  B I'm sorry. _____

6 **A** Excuse me! Where's the Regal Hotel?
  B I'm sorry. _____

Don't forget!

Grammar

14 Complete the chart.

Verb *to be*	Positive	Negative
I		*I'm not*
You		
He		*He isn't*
She	*is*	
It		
We	*are*	
They		

15 Write the correct answer.

1 **A** Hello, Peter.
  B __I'm not__ Peter. I'm Hans.
  a **I'm not**   b **I amn't**

2 **A** You and Daniella are from Russia, right?
  B _____ from Russia. We're from Slovakia.
  a **We no**   b **We aren't**

3 **A** Rome is in Spain, isn't it?
  B _____ in Spain! It's in Italy!
  a **It no is**   b **It isn't**

4 **A** Where's your phone?
  B _____ in my bag.
  a **Is**   b **It's**

5 She's French. _____ name's Antoinette.
  a **She's**   b **Her**

6 Hans is German. _____ from Berlin.
  a **His**   b **He's**

Prepositions

16 Write a preposition from the box.

in (x2) at (x2) from with of (x4) on

1 We're __at__ school now.
2 Emrah is Turkish. He's _____ Turkey.
3 The Empire State Building is _____ New York.
4 Moscow is the capital _____ Russia.
5 Hello. Can I have a cup _____ tea, please?
6 My brother is _____ holiday in Spain at the moment.
7 This is a photograph _____ me and my boyfriend.
8 My flat is _____ the centre _____ town.
9 Look _____ the park! It's so beautiful!
10 Read the interview _____ the band *Metro 5*.

Numbers

17 Write the number.

19	nineteen
____	twelve
____	twenty-one
____	seventy-five
____	fifty
____	fifteen
____	eight
____	forty-two
____	ten
____	thirty-eight

18 Write the number as a word.

31	thirty-one
45	_____
7	_____
68	_____
100	_____

in **at** **on** **with** **of** **from**

4

Possessive *'s* • *my / our / her...* • The family
• *has / have* • Vocabulary revision • The alphabet

Family and friends

Possessives

Possessive *'s*

1 Look at the picture. Complete the sentences with the names of the people + *'s*.

1 __Mike's__ car is a Mercedes.
2 _____ phone is on the table.
3 _____ computer is an Apple Mac.
4 _____ dictionary is on the table.

5 _____ office is in the centre of town.
6 _____ pizza looks fantastic!
7 _____ boyfriend is from Texas.
8 Ben is _____ dog.

my/our/her…

2 🎧 Complete the sentences with an adjective in the box.

your	~~My~~	His	Our	Their	Her

1 My _____ dog's name is Ben.

2 _____ boyfriend is from Texas.

3 _____ classroom is very small.

4 Is _____ car German?

5 _____ computer is really good!

6 _____ school is called Oxton College.

Vocabulary

The family

3 Look at the family tree. Complete the crossword with the name of the family relative.

James

Carrie

Dave   Petra   Belle

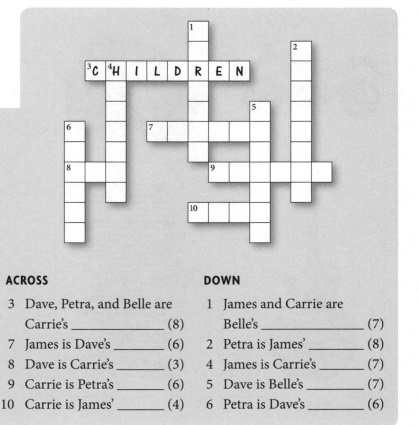

ACROSS

3 Dave, Petra, and Belle are Carrie's _____ (8)

7 James is Dave's _____ (6)

8 Dave is Carrie's _____ (3)

9 Carrie is Petra's _____ (6)

10 Carrie is James' _____ (4)

DOWN

1 James and Carrie are Belle's _____ (7)

2 Petra is James' _____ (8)

4 James is Carrie's _____ (7)

5 Dave is Belle's _____ (7)

6 Petra is Dave's _____ (6)

has/have

Alfie and his family

Ben　Archie　Penny　Kim　Alfie

Alfie	Kim

4 🎧 Look at the pictures. Complete the sentences about Alfie and his family.

1 _He has_ a BMW motorbike.
2 _They have_ a nice house.
3 _She_ a Canon camera.
4 _They_ two children.
5 _____ a lot of CDs.
6 _____ a guitar.
7 _____ a Mercedes.
8 _____ a Toshiba computer.
9 _____ a bicycle.

Listening

5 🎧 Listen to Alfie talking about his life and his family. Are the sentences true (✓) or false (✗)?

1 ✓ Kim is Alfie's wife.
2 ✗ Their house is very big.
3 ☐ He and Kim have a house in north London.
4 ☐ His sister, Alice, has a house in their street.
5 ☐ Alice has four children.
6 ☐ Alfie and Kim have two children and a cat.
7 ☐ Their daughter's name is Penny.
8 ☐ Kim's office is thirty miles from their house.
9 ☐ Alfie's office is in the centre.
10 ☐ Kim and Alfie aren't happy in their jobs.

6 Complete the questions.

1 What's _his wife's_ name? Kim
2 What's _____ name? Alice
3 What's _____ name? Penny
4 What's _____ name? Archie
5 What's _____ name? Ben

7 Complete the lines from Alfie talking about his life.

1 _Our_ house is nice, but it isn't very _big_ .
2 My sister, Alice, _____ a house in our street.
3 Our children and _____ children are at the same school.
4 The _____ school is near our house.
5 My _____ office is miles from our house.
6 _____ both happy in our jobs.

Reading

8 🎧 Read about these people. Use your dictionary. Answer the questions.

Who's happy?

Rich people are happy people.
True or false?

Roman Abramovich

Roman Abramovich is a businessman from Russia. He has $23.5 billion. He has five houses in London. He also has a farm in Colorado, USA, and a villa in the south of France. He has five yachts. He also has a lot of planes – a Boeing 767, an Airbus A340, and three helicopters. He has a lot of cars, too. And he has a football club, Chelsea FC.

He has five children. His girlfriend, Daria Zhukova, has a modern art gallery in Moscow.

He has a lot of problems. Is he happy?

Queen Elizabeth II

Queen Elizabeth II of England is one of the richest women in the world. She has $600 million. She has a house in Scotland, Balmoral, and a house in Sandringham, in the east of England. She has paintings by Leonardo da Vinci, Raphael, Vermeer, Canaletto, Rubens, Rembrandt, and Monet. She also has a lot of dogs and horses.

She has four children. Her husband, Prince Phillip, is from Greece. She has a lot of problems. Is she happy?

Tony and Abigail Jones

Tony has a house in London. 'Our house is small, but we love it. My wife's name is Abigail. We both have good jobs. Abigail's a police officer, and I'm a teacher. We have two children, Oliver and Jess, and their school is five minutes from our house. We have an old Renault car.'

'I have some money, but not a lot. Problems? Of course we have problems! Everyone has problems! But we're very happy!'

Are the sentences true (✓) or false (✗)?

Roman Abramovich

1 [✗] He is English.
2 [✓] He has lots of houses.
3 [ ] He has problems.

Queen Elizabeth

4 [ ] She has a house in America.
5 [ ] Her paintings are famous.
6 [ ] Her husband is Italian.

Tony and Abigail

7 [ ] They have a big house.
8 [ ] They have two children.
9 [ ] They're rich.

Vocabulary

Revision

9 Match a line in A with a line in B.

A	B
1 My dad is a big Chelsea	☐ a of England.
2 My sister's a student	☐ b CDs.
3 Catherine is my best	☐ c music.
4 Hip hop is my favourite	☐ d have a really good time.
5 I have a part-time	☐ e friend.
6 When I'm with my friends, we	☐ f at university.
7 Their house is in the north	☐1 g fan.
8 I have a lot of	☐ h job in a restaurant.

Pronunciation

they're or *their*?

10 *They're* and *their* sound the same /ðeə/. Complete the sentences with *they're* or *their*.

1 My children are happy because ___their___ friends are at the same school.
2 ___They're___ at school now.
3 _____ teachers are very good. Really fantastic.
4 _____ very nice with the children.
5 _____ school is small, and a bit old.
6 But _____ very happy in that school.

🎧 Listen and repeat.

Everyday English

The alphabet

11 🎧 Listen to a definition and then write the word.

> Your mother and father and brothers and sisters

f a m i l y

1 _ _ _ _ _ _ _
2 _ _ _ _ _ _ _
3 _ _ _ _
4 _ _ _
5 _ _ _ _ _ _ _ _
6 _ _ _ _ _ _ _
7 _ _ _ _ _
8 _ _ _ _ _ _ _

a b c d e
f g h i j k
l m n o p
q r s t u
v w x y z

On the phone

12 🎧 Listen. Complete the phone conversation.

A Good morning. The British Tourist Authority.
B Hello. Can you (1) _____ (2)_____ some information about hotels in London, (3)_____?
A Of course. (4)_____ name is . . . ?
B Alfonso Morelli.
A M O R R …
B No, no! M-O-R-E-double L-I. Just (5)_____ R .
A Thank you. And what's (6)_____ email address?
B amorelli@superdada.it
A I'll email you some (7)_____ today.
B That's (8)_____ kind. Thank you very (9)_____. Goodbye.
A My pleasure. Goodbye.

Don't forget!

Grammar

13 Complete the chart.

Pronouns	Adjectives
I	my
you	_____
he	his
she	_____
we	_____
they	their

14 Complete the chart of the verb *have*.

I	have
you	_____
he	
she	has
we	_____
they	_____

15 Write the correct answer.

1 I'm a student. __My__ school is very good.
   a **His**   b **My**

2 The school _____ fifteen classes.
   a **has**   b **have**

3 _____ teacher's name is Sarah.
   a **She's**   b **Our**

4 _____ from Canada.
   a **She's**   b **Her**

5 She _____ 23.
   a **is**   b **has**

6 She's French. _____ name's Antoinette.
   a **His**   b **Her**

your our his my her their

Vocabulary

16 Write the words in the correct column.

son	city	computer	accountant	town
bag	country	village	car	police officer
bus	sister	dictionary	waiter	apartment

Places	People	Things
city	son	computer

Singular and plural nouns

17 🎧 Complete the charts. Be careful about spellings.

Singular	Plural
brother	brothers
_____	jobs
school	_____
car	_____

Singular	Plural
country	countries
_____	families
city	_____
baby	_____

Singular	Plural
class	classes
address	_____
sandwich	_____
xxxx	sunglasses

Singular	Plural
man	men
_____	women
/wʊmən/	/wɪmɪn/
child	_____
person	_____

5

Sports/food/drink • Present Simple – *I/you/they*
• Languages and nationalities • *How much is it?*

Sports, food, drink

1 Look at the pictures and complete the crossword.

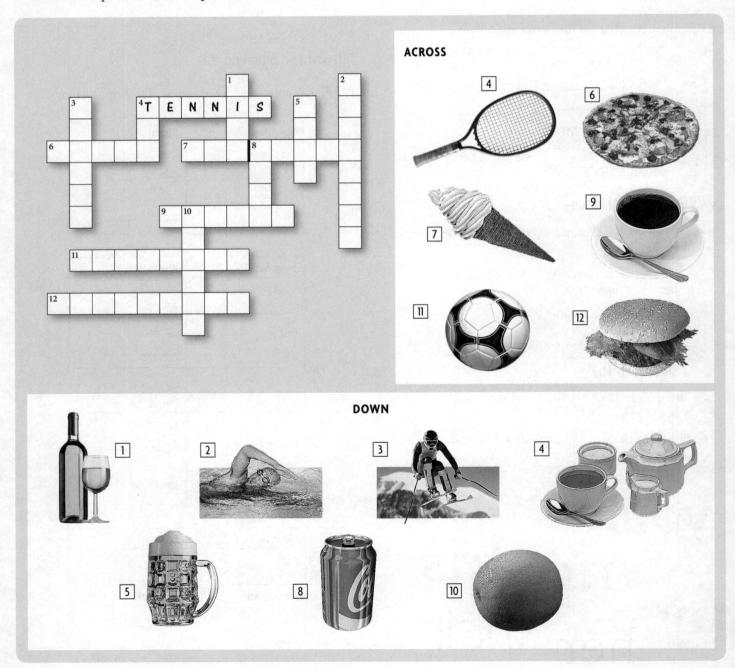

ACROSS

DOWN

Things I like

I like coffee

2 🎧 Write what the people like and don't like.

3 🎧 Write the questions and answers.

1 **A** <u>Do you like</u> Coke?
  B <u>Yes, I do. It's</u> great!

2 **A** <u>Do you like</u> football?
  B _____ . _____ terrible!

3 **A** _____ pizza?
  B _____ . _____ delicious!

4 **A** _____ skiing?
  B _____ . _____ fantastic!

5 **A** _____ James Bond films?
  B _____ . _____ exciting!

6 **A** _____ coffee?
  B _____ . _____ awful!

Present Simple

The swimmer Michael Phelps

4 Read and complete the text about Michael Phelps. Use the verbs in the box.

live	~~come~~	speak	have (x2)	eat
swim	drink	like	want	

THE BEST SWIMMER IN THE WORLD

Michael Phelps has 14 Olympic gold medals. He describes his life.

HOME 'I (1) _come_ from Baltimore, Maryland, USA. My father is a police officer, and my mother is a teacher. My parents are divorced. I (2) _____ two sisters, both older than me. I still (3) _____ in Baltimore. I (4) _____ my own apartment, but I (5) _____ to my mother on the phone every day.

TRAINING I train for six hours a day, six days a week. I (6) _____ 10 miles, that's 16 kilometres, every day. I (7) _____ a lot of pasta, omelettes, bread, cereal, sandwiches, cheese, pizza. In one day I eat enough for six people. I (8) _____ coffee and special energy drinks.

INTERESTS I (9) _____ football (American football, of course!), music (hip hop – Lil Wayne is my favourite), playing video games, and taking my dog, Herman, for a walk.

I (10) _____ to win 10 medals at the next Olympic games.'

Questions

5 Put the words in the right order to make questions about Michael Phelps.

1 come / Where / you / from / do
   Where do you come from _____?
   I come from Baltimore, Maryland.

2 father's / job / your / What's
   _____?
   He's a police officer.

3 you / live / Where / do
   _____?
   In an apartment in Baltimore.

4 eat / do / you / What
   _____?
   Pasta, omelettes, cereal … I eat a lot!

6 Complete the questions to Michael Phelps.

1 _What's your mother's job_ _____?
   She's a teacher.

2 How many sisters _____?
   Two.

3 What _____?
   Coffee and special energy drinks.

4 What sort of music _____?
   Hip hop.

Negatives

7 Make negative sentences.

1 I _don't eat_ a lot of meat, but I eat a lot of pasta.

2 I _____ beer or wine. I don't drink any alcohol.

3 I _____ with my family. I live in my own apartment.

4 My parents _____ together. They're divorced, so they live on their own.

5 My sisters _____ swim. They do other sports, but not swimming.

Listening

Gracie and her parents

8 🎧 Listen to Gracie Lloyd talking about her father and her mother. Complete the sentences.

1 Your parents __live__ in Spain, don't they?
2 That's right. _____ _____ a house in Seville.
3 They _____ a little Spanish, yes.
4 In Spain _____ _____ tennis.
5 You _____ in England, don't you?
6 _____ _____ a house in Scotland.
7 My _____ _____ to our house in summer.
8 _____ all _____ golf together.
9 _____ _____ golf!
10 We _____ at home. I love cooking.

9 Complete the questions from the interview.

1 __Do__ they __speak__ Spanish?

2 What _____ they _____ in Spain? _____ they play golf?

3 _____ _____ _____ still work?

4 Where _____ you and your husband _____ ?

5 And _____ _____ all _____ out to restaurants?

10 Complete the negative sentences from the interview.

1 They __don't live__ in England any more.
2 They're both quite old now, so they _____ _____ a lot.
3 _____ _____ work at all now.
4 We _____ _____ in England. We have a house in Scotland.
5 So _____ _____ _____ in restaurants.

Vocabulary

Languages and nationalities

11 Write the words in the box in the right column.

~~Japanese~~	Italian	~~English~~	Arabic
Chinese	Spanish	Brazilian	Mexican
American	German	Portuguese	

●●	●●	●●●	●●●	●●●●
English			**Japanese**	

🎧 Listen and repeat.

12 Complete the sentences with a nationality adjective.

1 Lisbon is a __Portuguese__ city.
2 The _____ President lives in the White House.
3 A Mercedes is a _____ car.
4 Nintendo is a _____ company.
5 كيف حالك is _____ writing.
6 Spaghetti is _____ food.
7 Tequila is a _____ drink.
8 Liu Xiuyan is a _____ name.
9 Ronaldinho is a _____ football player.
10 Real Madrid is a _____ football club.

Everyday English

How much is it?

13 Complete the numbers.

29 <u>twenty-nine</u>   ____ forty-eight   ____ thirty-five   81 _____   90 _____

____ fifteen   ____ seventy-two   60 _____   59 _____   100 _____

14 Match the prices and the words.

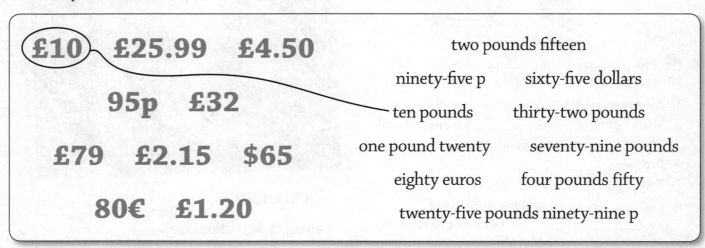

£10   £25.99   £4.50

95p   £32

£79   £2.15 $65

80€   £1.20

two pounds fifteen

ninety-five p   sixty-five dollars

ten pounds   thirty-two pounds

one pound twenty   seventy-nine pounds

eighty euros   four pounds fifty

twenty-five pounds ninety-nine p

15 🎧 Write the prices you hear.

1 <u>£10.99</u>   2 <u>$4.50</u>   3 _____   4 _____

5 _____   6 _____   7 _____   8 _____

16 🎧 Listen to the conversations. Write the prices.

1 <u>£15.75</u>   2 _____   3 _____   4 _____

5 _____   6 _____   7 _____   8 _____

Don't forget!

Grammar

17 Complete the chart.

Present simple

	Positive	Question	Negative
I	I work	Do I work?	
You			You don't work
We			
They		Do they work?	

18 Write the correct answer.

1 I __don't like__ French food.
   a **no like**   b **don't like**

2 'Do you like dancing?'   'Yes, _____.'
   a **I do**   b **I like**

3 How many languages _____?
   a **do you speak**   b **you speak**

4 I don't drink beer because I _____ it.
   a **like**   b **don't like**

5 In Brazil _____ Portuguese.
   a **speak**   b **they speak**

Vocabulary

19 Write the verb that goes with the words.

1 __live__ ◁ | in an apartment
             | with my parents

2 _____ ◁ | two languages
                 | to my mother on the phone

3 _____ ◁ | in a bank
                 | for an international company

4 _____ ◁ | two sisters
                 | a lot of money

5 _____ ◁ | the piano
                 | football

6 _____ ◁ | from the United States
                 | to school by bus

Articles *a / an*

20 Complete the sentences with *a* or *an*.

1 I'm in __an__ English class.
2 Hans is ____ waiter.
3 He wants to be ____ actor.
4 She has ____ Italian boyfriend.
5 A Mercedes is ____ German car.

21 Write *a* or *an* in the correct place in the sentence.

1 I have ⟋*a* good job.

2 We live in big house in London.

3 I'm waiter.

4 I work in Italian restaurant.

5 They have office in the centre of town.

6 Jamie is English teacher.

Word order

22 Put the words in the right order.

1 like   Spanish   I   oranges
   __I like Spanish oranges.__

2 have   small   I   flat   a
   _____

3 people   nice   are   Italian
   _____

4 food   don't   I   like   Chinese
   _____

5 job   father   important   has   an   My
   _____

do you speak...?

I don't like ...

6

The time • Present Simple – *he/she* • Prepositions *in/at/on*
• Words that go together • Days of the week

Every day

The time

1 🎧 <u>Underline</u> the correct time.

1 ten thirty / <u>ten fifteen</u>

2 three o' clock / five o' clock

3 eight thirty / nine thirty

4 six twenty-five / six forty-five

5 two forty-five / ten forty-five

6 eleven o' clock / twelve o' clock

2 🎧 Listen. Write the times you hear.

1 __1.15__   2 _____   3 _____   4 _____   5 _____

3 🎧 Listen and complete the conversations.

1 **A** Excuse __me__ ! What _____ is it?

   B It's _____ .

   A Thank _____ much.

   B That's OK.

2 **C** _____ me! Do _____
      the time, _____ ?

   D Sure. It's exactly _____ .

   C _____ a lot.

   D _____ all right.

Present Simple – *he/she*

Cathy and George

Cathy

George

4 🎧 Listen to Cathy and George.

Complete the questions and answers.

1 'What time _do you get up_____?'
  'I get up at _____,'

2 'What _____ for breakfast?'
  'I have toast and coffee.'

3 'How _____ to school?'
  'By bus.'

4 'What _____ in the evening?'
  'I _____ TV.'

5 Complete the verbs.

1	I get	→	He **gets**
2	You go	→	She **goes**
3	We have	→	He
4	I leave	→	She
5	We do	→	He
6	You watch	→	She
7	They live	→	He
8	I work	→	She

6 Complete the sentences about Cathy and George.

1 Cathy _gets up____ at 7.00 and _____ a shower.

2 She _____ to school by bus.

3 She _____ a sandwich and a Coke for lunch.

4 She _____ school at 3.30.

5 In the evening she _____ her homework.

6 George _____ in a house in north London.

7 He _____ toast and coffee for breakfast.

8 In the evening he _____ TV.

Questions

7 🎧 Complete the questions about Cathy and George.

Cathy

1 What time _does Cathy get up_____?
  At 7.00.

2 How _____ to school?
  By bus.

3 What _____ for lunch?
  A sandwich and a Coke.

4 What _____ in the evening?
  She does her homework.

George

5 Where _____ George _____?
  In a house in north London.

6 What _____ for breakfast?
  Toast and coffee.

7 Where _____ work?
  In a bank.

8 What _____ in the evening?
  He watches TV.

Cathy's bedroom

8 Look at Cathy's bedroom. Complete the sentences about her.

1 Cathy __has__ a lot of clothes.

2 She _____ her homework in her room.

3 _____ a boy called Max.

4 _____ shopping a lot.

5 _____ coffee.

6 _____ music.

7 _____ the guitar.

8 _____ pizza.

9 _____ fashion magazines.

9 Make negative sentences about Cathy.

1 She __doesn't__ tidy her room.

2 She _____ smoke.

3 She _____ like school.

4 Her parents _____ go in her room.

5 She _____ eat meat.

do/does/am/is/are

10 🎧 Complete the sentences with *do/does/am/is/are*.

A (1) __Are__ you Cathy's brother?

B Yes, I (2) _____ .

A Ah! (3) _____ your name Robert?

B Yes, it (4) _____ , but people call me Bobby.
(5) _____ you know my sister?

A Yes. I (6)_____ . My name (7) _____ Alice.

B (8) _____ you go to the same school?

A Yes, we (9) _____ . We (10) _____ in
the same class. I think I know your father, too.
(11) _____ he work in Barclays Bank?

B Yes, he (12) _____ . You know all the family!

Pronunciation

-s at the end of a word

11 🎧 Listen and write the verbs in the correct column for the pronunciation of -s at the end of the word.

~~goes~~	~~gets~~	~~watches~~	lives	eats	does
cooks	has	plays	listens	works	teaches

/z/	/s/	/ɪz/
goes	gets	watches

Prepositions

in/at/on

12 Complete the sentences with the correct preposition – *in*, *at*, or *on*.

1 I get up __at__ 7.00.
2 I don't work _____ Tuesday.
3 I get up late _____ the weekend.
4 _____ the evening I watch TV.
5 I don't like getting up _____ Monday morning.
6 I start work _____ 8.30.
7 I usually go to the cinema _____ Friday evening.

Do we need a preposition in these sentences?

8 I have a shower _____ every morning.
9 Come and see me _____ next weekend.
10 Are you at home _____ this evening?

Vocabulary

Words that go together

13 Think of a word that goes in the space.

• have toast for __breakfast__
• __drink__ beer

Complete the crossword.

Across

4 have toast for _____ (9)
6 _____ beer (5)
7 _____ TV (5)
8 _____ football (4)
9 _____ a car (5)
10 have _____ at 1.00 (5)
12 speak two _____ (9)
13 get up _____ / get up late (5)

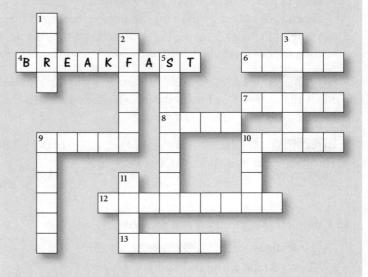

Down

1 _____ for an American company (4)
2 work in an _____ (6)
3 _____ to music (6)
5 go _____ to buy things (7)
9 cook _____ in the evening (6)
10 _____ in a flat (4)
11 _____ two sisters (4)

Reading

14 🎧 Read the newspaper article about Barack Obama. Use your dictionary.

Barack Obama, America's first black President

BARACK OBAMA is the forty-fourth President of the United States, but the first African American President in the history of the country. He was born in Hawaii in 1961. His father was a black Kenyan, and his mother a white American from Kansas.

His family He is married to Michelle, and they have two daughters, Malia Anne and Natasha, known as Sasha. The children go to a private school in Washington. The girls have a dog called Bo.

Michelle is an attorney (an American lawyer). She doesn't work now her husband is President. She says her most important job is as mother to their children.

His interests Barack Obama loves basketball. He has his own indoor basketball court in the White House, and he often invites professional basketball players to come and play with him.

He also goes to the gym. In the evening he sometimes plays billiards. He and Michelle like going to restaurants and the cinema, and visiting friends for dinner. The family goes to church every Sunday.

His home The President and his family live in the White House. It has 132 rooms. One hundred people work for him. His chefs make his favourite food – chilli and pasta.

His work Mr Obama works in the Oval Office in the White House. He often works more than sixteen hours a day.

15 Complete the questions and answers.

1 How many _children does he have_ ?
   Two – Malia Anne and Sasha.

2 Where _____ to school?
   They go to a private school in Washington.

3 What _____ Michelle _____?
   She looks after their children.

4 What sport _____ like?
   Basketball.

5 Where _____ work?
   In the Oval Office.

6 How many hours _____?
   About sixteen.

16 Complete the short answers.

1 Do the children have a dog?
   ___Yes___ , ___they do___

2 Does Michelle work as a lawyer now?
   _____ , _____

3 Does he play basketball?
   _____ , _____

4 Do they go to church?
   _____ , _____

17 Make negative sentences.

1 His children _don't go to state school_ .
2 Mrs Obama _____ go out to work.
3 They _____ live in Chicago.
4 The President _____ a lot of free time.

Everyday English

Days of the week

18 Write the days of the week in the correct order.

~~**Monday**~~

Wednesday   Monday _____

Friday   _____

Saturday   _____

Sunday   _____

Tuesday   _____

Thursday

Don't forget!

Present Simple

19 Complete the chart.

	Positive	Question	Negative
I	I work	Do I work?	
You			You don't work
He		Does he work?	
She	She works		
It			It doesn't work

20 Add -s, -es, or – (nothing).

1 My brother love _s_ football.
2 Tom and Julia often go _-_ shopping.
3 Susan watch___ videos every evening.
4 James cook___ dinner in the evening.
5 We work___ late on Tuesday evening.
6 Ellie teach___ English at my school.

21 Underline the correct word.

1 *Do / Does* you like hip hop?
2 Where *do / does* your sister live?
3 What languages *do / does* your teacher speak?
4 *Do / Does* you have a computer at home?
5 I *don't / doesn't* get up early at the weekend.
6 My parents *don't / doesn't* like my boyfriend.

Questions

22 Match a question with a question word.

~~What~~	When	How	How much
How many	Where	Who	

1 __What__ do you do in the evening? – I watch TV.
2 _____ do you come to school? – By bus.
3 _____ is a cup of coffee? – 90p.
4 _____ are you from? – I'm from Spain.
5 _____ is your teacher? – Sally.
6 _____ do you go on holiday? – In summer.
7 _____ languages do you speak? – Two.

Articles: *the* or – (nothing)?

23 Complete the sentences with *the* or – (nothing).

1 The Empire State Building is in __-__ New York.
2 New York is in _____ United States.
3 _____ Paris is _____ capital of _____ France.
4 Excuse me! What's _____ time?
5 I have _____ lunch at 1.00 every day.
6 I go to _____ work by _____ bus.
7 I go to _____ bed at 11.30.
8 What's _____ name of your school?
9 In _____ evening I watch _____ TV.
10 At _____ weekend I play _____ football.

how

when

what

who

where

7

Questions • Pronouns *me / him* • Possessive adjectives *my/his*
• *this / that* • Adjectives *happy / miserable* • *Can I . . . ?*

My favourites

Questions

An interview with Johnny Depp

1 Read and complete the interview with Johnny Depp. Use the questions in the box.

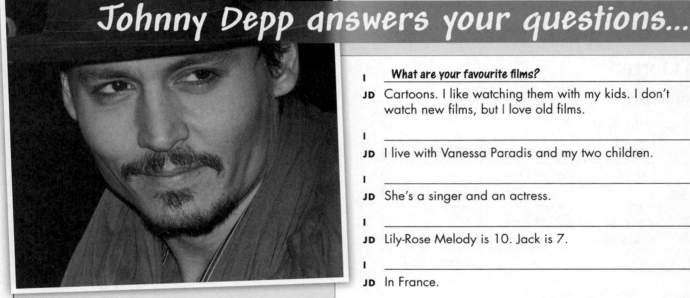

Johnny Depp answers your questions...

I **What are your favourite films?**

JD Cartoons. I like watching them with my kids. I don't watch new films, but I love old films.

I _____

JD I live with Vanessa Paradis and my two children.

I _____

JD She's a singer and an actress.

I _____

JD Lily-Rose Melody is 10. Jack is 7.

I _____

JD In France.

I _____

JD Because Vanessa is French. And because I feel at home in France. I go to the café with my daughter and have a coffee, and no one looks at us.

I _____

JD Two. English and French.

I _____

JD I play the guitar.

I _____

JD I drive a green Porsche convertible. I also have a Triumph motorbike.

I _____

JD That's private. I have a lot. I make money doing what I like. I'm very lucky.

What are your favourite films?

Why do you live in France?

How many languages do you speak?

Who do you live with?

How old are your children?

Where do you live?

What does Vanessa do?

What car do you drive?

How much money do you have?

Do you play any musical instruments?

Question words

2 Match a question word in **A** with an answer in **B**.

A	B
1 What?	☐ a In the summer.
2 Where?	☐1 b A sandwich.
3 Who?	☐ c By bus.
4 When?	☐ d Because my wife is French.
5 How?	☐ e In a village near the sea.
6 Why?	☐ f Jane.
7 How old?	☐ g Three.
8 How many?	☐ h I'm twenty-one.
9 What time?	☐ i 6.30 in the morning.
10 How much?	☐ j £5.30.

3 🎧 Complete the questions with a question word from **A** in exercise 2. Write in the answer from **B**.

1 __What__ do you have for lunch?

   __A sandwich__ .

2 _____ is your next holiday?

   _____

3 _____ do you come to school?

   _____

4 _____ do you live?

   _____

5 _____'s your teacher?

   _____

6 _____ do you live in France?

   _____

7 _____ are you?

   I'm twenty-one.

8 _____ brothers do you have?

   _____

9 _____ do you start work?

   _____

10 _____ is a coffee and a sandwich?

   _____

4 🎧 Write questions for these answers.

1 __What's your email address__ ?

   jharman@btinternet.com

2 _____ spell _____ surname?

   H - A - R - M - A - N.

3 _____ ?

   07933 678234.

4 _____ ?

   I'm 23.

5 _____ favourite _____ ?

   Pizza. I love it.

6 _____ in a house or a flat?

   A flat.

Why? Because. . .

5 Write questions with *Why?* and then choose a reason from the box.

> Because she works at home.
> ~~Because he has a job there.~~
> Because he doesn't have any money.
> Because she's a writer.

1 Mike lives in Moscow.

   __Why does he live in Moscow__ ?

   __Because he has a job there.__

2 He drives an old car.

   Why _____ ?

   _____

3 Sally stays at home every day.

   Why _____ ?

   _____

4 She sits at her computer for ten hours a day.

   Why _____ ?

   _____

Pronouns and possessives

me / him; my / his

6 Complete the chart.

Subject	Object	Possessive
I	*me*	*my*
You	*you*	*your*
He		
She	*her*	
It		*its*
We		
They		*their*

7 Complete the sentences with *me, you, him, her, it, us, them*.

1 **A** John, do you like __me__?
   B Of course I like __you__! I love _____!

2 Maria's English isn't very good. I don't understand _____.

3 Daddy! Look at _____! I'm on the table!

4 **A** My coffee's cold!
   B Don't drink _____!

5 I don't like Mike. Please don't invite _____ to your party.

6 **A** Is this a photo of _____?
   B Yes. I was on holiday in Spain.

7 **A** Peter, I want to speak to _____.
   B Phone_____ later.

8 Our teacher gives _____ too much homework!

9 My neighbours are so loud! Listen to _____!

10 You're so horrible sometimes! Stop _____!

8 Complete the sentences with *my, your, his, hers, its, our, their*.

1 Alice, this is __my__ wife. Kay, this is Alice.

2 **A** Peter, what's _____ email address?
   B petersmith@hotmail.com

3 James is an actor. _____ son's an actor, too.

4 Sue's a doctor. _____ daughter's a doctor, too.

5 The dog eats _____ food, then it eats the cat's food.

6 _____ teacher gives us too much homework!

7 My children don't like _____ teachers, but I think they're great.

this / that

9 🎧 Complete the conversations with *this* or *that*.

1 **A** Who's __that__?
   B Her name's Lola.

2 **A** What's __this__?
   B It's tomato soup.

3 **A** I love _____ car!
   B It's great, isn't it!

4 **A** _____ letter's for you.
   B Oh! Thanks.

5 **J** Hi, Larry. _____ is James. How are you?

6 **A** How much is _____ coat? The black one.

Vocabulary

Adjectives – *happy*/*miserable*

10 <u>Underline</u> the correct word.

Happy Annie

Annie is very (1) *old* / <u>*happy*</u>. It's Saturday, she doesn't work today, and the weather is (2) *lovely* / *awful*. It's summer, and it's (3) *cold* / *hot*.

   She's in the park. The park is very (4) *right* / *big*. A lot of people have (5) *hot* / *delicious* picnics. The flowers are (6) *beautiful* / *terrible*.

   Annie wants an ice cream. 'How much is an ice cream?' '20p.' 'Wow! That's (7) *cheap* / *expensive*!'

   Annie and her friends love the park. 'It's (8) *horrible* / *wonderful* here!' says Annie.

Miserable Mike

Mike is very miserable. It's Monday morning, and it's time for work. The weather is (1) *big* / *terrible*. It's winter, and it's (2) *nice* / *wet* outside.

   It's 6.30 in the morning, and Mike feels (3) *great* / *awful*. He's tired. His flat is very (4) *old* / *new*, and the heating isn't very good, so it's (5) *hot* / *cold* in winter.

   The flat is £1,000 a week, so it is very (6) *cheap* / *expensive*. And there is only one bedroom, so the flat is very (7) *small* / *big*, too.

   This is why Mike isn't (8) *happy* / *great*.

Everyday English

Can I ...?

11 🎧 Write a line from the box in the correct place.

1 In a café

| How much is that? | ~~have a cup of tea~~ |
| Anything to eat? | chocolate cake |

A Can I __have a cup of tea__, please?

B Sure. _____?

A Yes. Can I have a piece of _____?

B Of course. Here you are.

A _____?

B That's £4.60, please.

2 In a clothes shop

| Can I try it on | Do you have this T-shirt |
| over there | Certainly |

C _____ in a medium, please?

D I'll have a look for you.

C Thanks.

D Yes. Here you are.

C Oh! Thank you. _____ please?

D _____. The changing rooms

are _____.

3 In a train station

| have a ticket | Can I pay by credit card |
| a single | enter your PIN |

C Can I _____ to Brighton, please?

D Do you want _____ or a return?

C A single, please.

D That's £25.50, please.

C _____?

D Sure. Put your card in the machine.

And _____. Now take your card.

Don't forget!

Vocabulary

12 Look at the pictures and complete the crossword. All the words are in Unit 7 of the Student's Book.

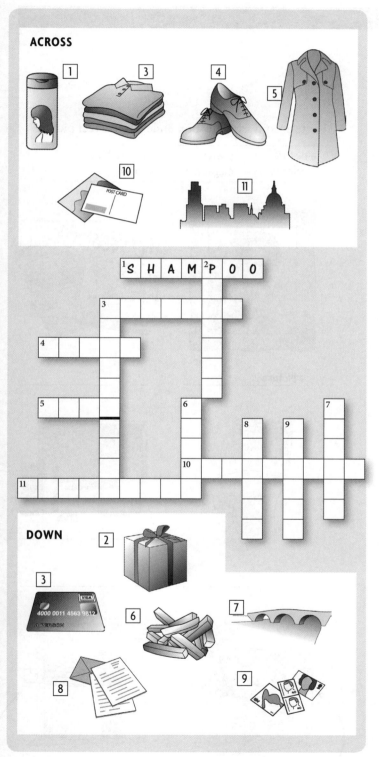

ACROSS

¹S H A M ²P O O

DOWN

Grammar

13 Write the correct answer.

1 _How much_ money do you have?
   a **How much**   b **How many**

2 _____ do you live in London?
   Because I like it.
   a **When**   b **Why**

3 _____ is your favourite actor?
   Johnny Depp.
   a **Who**   b **How**

4 Pete is great. I like _____ very much.
   a **him**   b **his**

5 My sister has a flat. I live with _____ .
   a **she**   b **her**

6 They aren't your books! They're my books!
   Give _____ !
   a **they me**   b **them to me**

Prepositions

14 Complete the sentences with a preposition from the box.

of	to	with	for	at	in

1 Jane's married __to__ Pete.
2 What do you do _____ your free time?
3 I have a present _____ you.
4 Look _____ that photo! Is that you?
5 In the evening I listen _____ music.
6 Can I speak _____ you, please?
7 This is a photo _____ me with my boyfriend.
8 Thank you _____ my present.
9 We go _____ a restaurant _____ a pizza.
10 I live _____ my mother and sisters.

its   them
it   me
their   my

8

Rooms and furniture • *There is*/there *are*
• Prepositions *on/under/next to* . . .
• Vocabulary revision • Directions

Where I live

Rooms and furniture

1 🎧 Complete the sentences with a room in the house.

1 We eat in the <u>dining room.</u>
2 We relax and watch TV in the _____
3 We cook in the _____
4 I have a shower in the _____
5 I sleep in my _____

2 Tick (✓) the correct word.

1 We keep milk in the
  [✓] fridge.
  [ ] shower.

2 I sleep in my
  [ ] desk.
  [ ] bed.

3 We cook lunch on the
  [ ] cooker.
  [ ] fridge.

4 I sit on the
  [ ] laptop
  [ ] sofa
  when I watch TV.

5 I do my homework at my
  [ ] desk.
  [ ] lamp.

6 We sit at the
  [ ] desk
  [ ] table
  when we have lunch.

7 I play games on my
  [ ] DVD player.
  [ ] laptop.

8 Our dog always sits in my father's
  [ ] armchair.
  [ ] bag.

3 Write a word from the box under the correct picture.

a picture	posters	a PlayStation®
a balcony	magazines	a toilet

1   <u>a picture</u>   2 _____

3 _____   4 _____

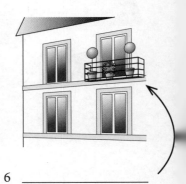

5 _____   6 _____

There is / There are

In the garden

4 Look at the picture. Are the sentences true (✔) or false (✗)?

1 ✔ There are two boys playing football.
2 ✗ There's a PlayStation® in the living room.
3 ☐ There's a table in the kitchen.
4 ☐ There are three lamps in the living room.
5 ☐ There's a desk in the living room.
6 ☐ There's a cooker in the kitchen.

5 🎧 Complete the sentences with *There's* or *There are*.

1 **There's** a table in the garden.
2 _____ two women sitting at the table.
3 _____ a pot of tea on the table.
4 _____ a dog in the garden.
5 _____ two people cooking in the kitchen.
6 _____ a sofa in the living room.

6 🎧 Make negative sentences with *There isn't* or *There aren't*.

1 **There aren't** any posters on the walls.
2 _____ a cat in the house.
3 _____ any flowers in the garden.
4 _____ a Play station® in the living room.
5 _____ any people in the living room.
6 _____ a DVD player.

7 🎧 Complete the questions and answers.

1 Is there a balcony?
   No, there isn't.

2 _____ a girl in the garden?
   _____

3 _____ any armchairs in the living room?
   _____

4 _____ any children in the house?
   _____

Prepositions

on/under/next to...

8 Where are the things? Write sentences.

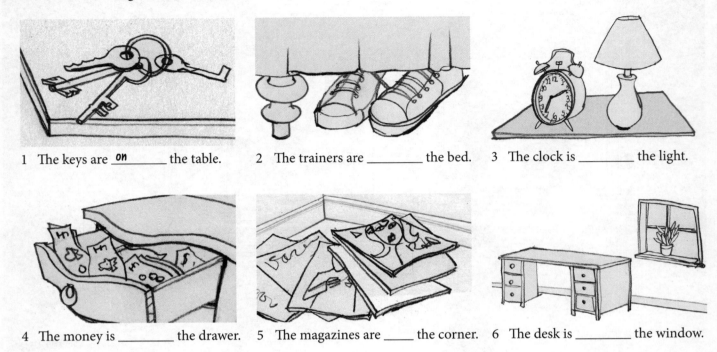

1   The keys are __on__ the table.

2   The trainers are _____ the bed.

3   The clock is _____ the light.

4   The money is _____ the drawer.

5   The magazines are ____ the corner.

6   The desk is _____ the window.

Vocabulary

Revision – Vancouver

9 Look at the pictures and complete the crossword. All the words are in the reading text on p60–61 of the Student's Book.

Everyday English

Directions

10 Look at the map of Appleby. Write the places in the box on the map.

park	~~newsagent's~~	railway station
church	sports centre	car park
supermarket	chemist's	

11 🎧 Listen to the directions. Start from YOU ARE HERE. Follow the directions. Where are you?

Go down the High Street. Turn left into Albion Road. It's on the right, next to the Chinese restaurant. Where are you?

The newsagent's

1 _____
2 _____
3 _____
4 _____
5 _____

12 🎧 Listen and complete the conversations.

1 **A** Excuse me! Is there a bank near here?
  B Yes. _____ straight on. It's on the _____, next to the _____.
  A Thanks a lot.

2 **C** Excuse me! How do I get to the railway station?
  D Go down the High Street. Turn _____. Go down _____ Road. It's near the bridge, on the _____.
  C That's very kind. Thank you.

3 **E** Excuse me! How _____ the sports centre?
  F Go _____ Street. Go past the post office, past School Lane. It's _____ right, _____ the cinema.
  E Thank you very much.

4 **G** Excuse me! _____ a supermarket _____?
  H Yes. Turn _____ into Riverside. It's on _____ next to the _____, near the river.
  G Thanks. Bye!

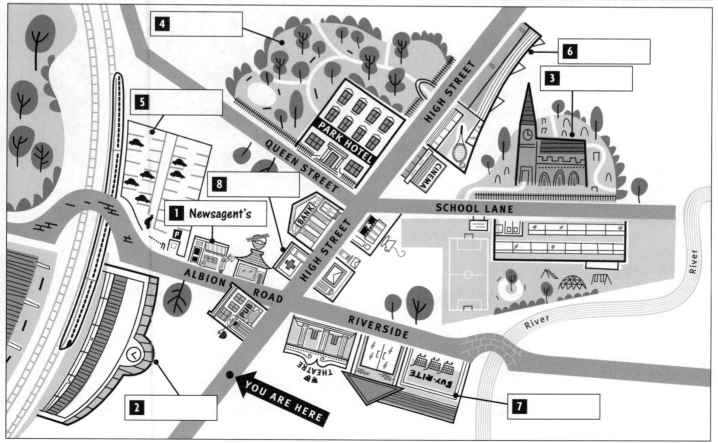

Reading

13 🎧 Read about the town of Berkhamsted. Are these sentences true (✓) or false (✗)? Correct the false sentences.

Berkhamsted
OFFICIAL GUIDE

DESCRIPTION Berkhamsted is a historic market town 20 miles north of London. It has a population of 19,000, and is in the middle of beautiful English countryside.

PLACES OF INTEREST The Castle is more than 1,000 years old. It is open every day, and it is free.

The Ashridge Estate is a huge park with woods, views, and walks. There is a shop and a café.

TRAVEL There are four trains an hour into London. The journey takes 30–40 minutes.

HOTELS There are several hotels in the town. The biggest are the King's Arms Hotel and the Pennyfarthing Hotel, both in the High Street.

SHOPS There is everything you need in the High Street and Lower Kings Road. You will find chemists, bookshops, specialist food shops, clothes shops, bakers, dry cleaners – all the usual high street shops.

RESTAURANTS AND CAFES You will find French, Italian, Thai, and Indian restaurants.

There are also coffee bars and tea rooms on the High Street.

MARKET There is a street market every Saturday.

SUPERMARKETS The town has two big supermarkets, Waitrose and Tesco.

CINEMA The Rex Cinema is in a luxurious 1930s building.

PUBS *The Bull* and *The Crown* on the High Street. *The Boat* is next to the canal.

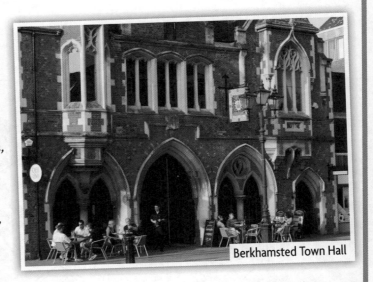
Berkhamsted Town Hall

1 ✗ The castle is 2,000 years old.
   The castle is 1,000 years old.

2 ✓ There is a park called the Ashridge Estate.

3 ☐ There are six trains an hour into London.

4 ☐ It takes an hour to get into London from Berkhamsted.

5 ☐ There's only one hotel in the town.

6 ☐ You can buy things to eat, read, and wear.

7 ☐ There are Mediterranean and Asian restaurants.

8 ☐ There's a market one day a week.

9 ☐ There's a theatre, but there isn't a cinema.

10 ☐ There are a lot of pubs on the High Street.

Don't forget!

Vocabulary and grammar

14 Write the correct answer.

1 You can get a __train__ at a railway station.
  a **bus**　　b **train**

2 My brother's a _____
  a **cook**　　b **cooker**

3 You can buy books in a _____
  a **library**　　b **bookshop**

4 A laptop is a small _____
  a **computer**　　b **DVD player.**

5 _____ fifteen students in my class.
  a **There are**　　b **Are**

6 _____ a chemist's near here?
  a **Is**　　b **Is there**

7 Paul! Come on! Your lunch is _____ the table.
  a **next to**　　b **on**

8 Where are my car keys? Are they _____ the drawer?
  a **in**　　b **under**

And and but

15 Look at the sentences with *and* and *but*.
I like wine and I like beer. ☺
I like Peter, but I don't like his wife. ☹

Complete the sentences with *and* or *but*.

1 I have a house in the country __and__ I have a flat in London.

2 I love the house, _____ my neighbours are horrible.

3 I have two jobs. I work in a café _____ I'm a taxi driver.

4 I want to go shopping, _____ I don't have any money.

So and because

16 Look at the sentences with *so* and *because*.
I like my job because it's interesting.
He has a lot of problems, so he isn't very happy.

Complete the sentences with *so* or *because*.

1 I start work at 5 in the morning, __so__ I go to bed early.

2 I like my job _____ I have a lot of friends there.

3 I want to marry you _____ I love you. That's why.

4 I want to be a professional tennis player, _____ I practise every day.

Numbers

17 Write the numbers.

_15_	fifteen	____	thirteen
____	eight	____	twelve
____	thirty	____	fifty-eight
____	twenty-five	____	nine
____	sixty	____	forty-two

18 Write the numbers as words.

36	_thirty-six_
4	_____
72	_____
88	_____
10	_____

go down

next to

turn right

on the left

9

Saying years • *was/were* • Past Simple – irregular verbs
• *have/do/go* • Months and dates

Times past

Saying years

1 🎧 Listen and match the years.

1	2006	two thousand and twenty (twenty twenty)
2	2000	two thousand and six
3	2010	two thousand and ten (twenty ten)
4	2015	two thousand
5	2020	two thousand and fifteen (twenty fifteen)

6	1995	nineteen eighty-two
7	1990	nineteen sixteen
8	1982	nineteen ninety
9	1960	nineteen ninety-five
10	1916	nineteen sixty

2 🎧 Listen and write the years.

1 __2009__   4 _____
2 _____   5 _____
3 _____   6 _____

3 Write the years in words.

1 1985   _nineteen eighty-five_
2 1940   _____
3 1999   _____
4 1973   _____
5 2001   _____
6 2005   _____
7 2008   _____
8 2012   _____

4 🎧 Do the *Dates Quiz*. Choose a year from the box.

1969	1989	1963	2004	1945

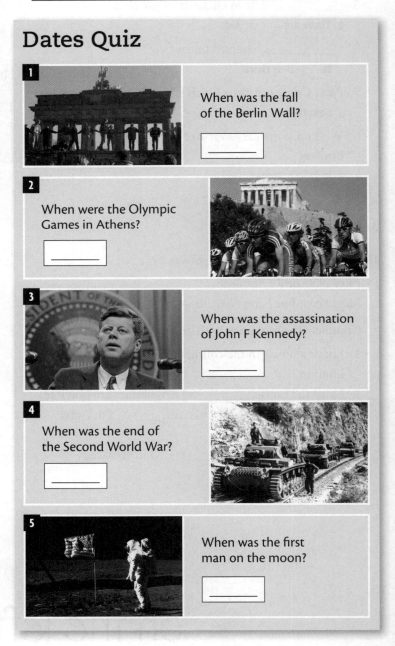

Dates Quiz

1 When was the fall of the Berlin Wall?

_____

2 When were the Olympic Games in Athens?

_____

3 When was the assassination of John F Kennedy?

_____

4 When was the end of the Second World War?

_____

5 When was the first man on the moon?

_____

was/were

Tom

was born

5 🎧 Listen to Tom. Complete the sentences.

1 My mother **was born** in Chicago in 1960.
2 My father _____ in New York in 1958.
3 I _____ in 1985.
4 My grandparents _____ in the United States.
5 My mother's parents _____ in Sweden.
6 My father's parents _____ in Ireland.

6 🎧 Listen to Tom saying more about his relatives. Complete the sentences.

1 My mother _____ a pharmacist.
2 My father _____ a professor.
3 They _____ at university together.
4 My father's parents _____ very poor.
5 My mother's parents _____ married in Sweden. They met in the States.
6 Grandpa Fredrik _____ an engineer.
7 Grandma Smilla _____ a piano teacher.
8 Pat and Paddy _____ happy at first. Life _____ very hard for them.

Questions

7 Complete the questions.

1 Where **was** Tom's mother **born**?
   In Chicago.
2 When _____ _____ _____?
   In 1960.
3 Where _____ his mother's parents _____?
   In Sweden.
4 What _____ Fredrik's job?
   He was an engineer.

Negatives

8 Complete the negative sentences.

1 Tom's mother **wasn't born** in Sweden.
2 His father _____ in Ireland.
3 His grandparents _____ in the United States.
4 'Were Pat and Paddy happy at first?'
   'No, they _____.'

53

Reading

9 🎧 Read about Andy Warhol and Princess Diana. Use your dictionary.

Andy Warhol
1928–1987

Andy Warhol was an American painter and filmmaker. He was famous for his pictures of everyday things, like tins of soup and Coca-Cola bottles, and portraits of celebrities such as Marilyn Monroe.

He was born in Pittsburgh, Pennsylvania. His parents were born in Slovakia and immigrated to the US in 1914. His father was a coal miner. The family were Catholic, and Warhol was religious all his life.

As a child, Andy Warhol was often ill, and was not at school for a long time. He was a student of art in Pittsburgh. In 1949 he went to New York. Here he was a painter in advertising and magazines.

In the 1960s he started The Factory, a centre for artists, musicians, and writers.

All his life Warhol was afraid of doctors and hospitals. He died in a hospital in New York after an operation.

Princess Diana
1961–1997

Princess Diana was the first wife of Charles, Prince of Wales.

She was born in Sandringham, England. Her father was John, Earl Spencer, and her mother was Frances, Viscountess Althorp. They were both friends of the Royal family. Her parents divorced in 1969. She wasn't a happy child.

Diana was at a lot of schools, but she wasn't a good student. In London she was a dance teacher and a teacher in a children's school. She met Prince Charles in 1980 at a party.

She was 20 years old when she married Prince Charles. She had two sons, William and Harry, but her marriage wasn't happy. She and Charles divorced in 1996. After her divorce, Diana was very busy with charity work, visiting hospitals and poor countries in Africa.

She died in a car accident in Paris in August 1997. She was with Dodi Al-Fayed.

Answer the questions about Andy Warhol.

1 What was he famous for?
2 Where was he born?
3 Where were his parents from?
4 What was his father's job?
5 Was he a healthy child?
6 What was his job in New York?
7 What was The Factory?
8 What was he afraid of?

Answer the questions about Princess Diana.

1 Where was she born?
2 Who were her parents?
3 Who were her parents' friends?
4 Was she a happy child?
5 What was her job in London?
6 How old was she when she married Charles?
7 Where was she when she died?
8 Who was she with?

Past Simple

Irregular verbs

10 Write in the Past Simple form of these verbs.

1 go __went__   2 is _____   3 are _____
4 buy _____   5 say _____   6 find _____
7 think _____   8 come _____   9 see _____

11  Complete the story with an irregular verb in the Past Simple.

Vocabulary

have / do / go

12 Complete the sentences with a word that goes with *have / do / go*. They are on page 70 of the Student's Book. Do the crossword.

ACROSS

2 We went on _____ to Spain. (7)

3 It's late and I'm tired. I want to go _____ now. (4)

4 It was a lovely day so I went for a _____ with my dog. (4)

9 I went _____ yesterday and I bought a new jumper. (8)

10 I have a _____ every morning, not a bath. (6)

11 I go to the gym every day. I like to do some _____ . (8)

² H O L I D A Y

DOWN

1 The party was great! Everyone had a good _____ . (4)

3 I did some _____ because my flat was so messy. (9)

5 I have _____ at my desk at 1.00. I have a sandwich. (5)

6 This morning I had _____ at 7.00. I had toast and cereal. (9)

7 I went to _____ early yesterday. The office was quiet. (4)

8 I do my _____ with my dictionary and this Workbook. (8)

Everyday English

Months and dates

13 Write in the missing months in the calendar from the box.

June	~~February~~	December
August	April	October

January	February	March
_____	May	_____
July	_____	September
_____	November	_____

14 Match the words and numbers.

first — 7th
second 12th
third 1st
fourth 5th
fifth 21st
seventh 3rd
tenth 2nd
twelfth 20th
twentieth 4th
twenty-first 10th

15 🎧 Listen and <u>underline</u> the date you hear.

1 8 March / <u>18 April</u>

2 2 June / 22 July

3 3 September / 3 November

4 15 January / 15 February

5 10 May / 20 June

6 25 December / 16 August

Don't forget!

Grammar

16 Complete the chart.

Verb _to be_ in the Past Simple

	Positive	Negative
I	was	
You		weren't
He / She		
We	were	
They		weren't

17 Write the correct answer.

1 Ayrton Senna __was__ a racing driver.
   a **be**   b **was**

2 I _____ born in Paris in 1978.
   a **was**   b **am**

3 Where _____ you yesterday?
   a **was**   b **were**

4 You _____ at school. Were you ill?
   a **no were**   b **weren't**

5 My sister and I _____ happy as children.
   a **were**   b **was**

6 The Beatles _____ American. They were English.
   a **wasn't**   b **weren't**

Vocabulary

18 Complete the chart.

Present	Past
go	went
have	
	did
see	
buy	
	said
find	
	came
make	

19 Complete the sentences with _did_ or _made_.

1 Exercise 1 was easy, so I __did__ exercises 2 and 3.
2 Andy Warhol __made__ a lot of films.
3 I _____ dinner last night. It was delicious.
4 You _____ a lot of mistakes in your homework. Do it again!
5 I _____ a lot of work yesterday. I'm very tired today.
6 Do you like this cake? I _____ it.

Word order

20 Write the word on the right in the correct place in the sentence.

1 I born in Scotland.   **was**
   <u>I was born in Scotland.</u>

2 I went to cinema last night.   **the**
   _____

3 I my homework before I go to bed.   **do**
   _____

4 I like school because is interesting.   **it**
   _____

5 I have shower, then I have breakfast.   **a**
   _____

6 'What you do?' 'I'm businessman.'   **do / a**
   _____

7 I have tea for breakfast.   **usually**
   _____

was   wasn't
weren't   were

10

Past Simple – regular verbs • Questions and negatives
• Making conversation • Sport and leisure activities
• Going sightseeing

We had a great time!

Past Simple

Regular verbs

1 Write the Past Simple of these regular verbs.

play	→	played	like	→	liked
watch	→		live	→	
want	→		phone	→	
listen	→		visit	→	
start	→		love	→	
work	→		stay	→	

Pronunciation

2 🎧 Write the Past Simple of the verbs in exercise 1 in the correct column for the pronunciation of -ed.

/t/	/d/	/ɪd/
watched	played	wanted

Listen and repeat.

Irregular verbs

3 Write the Past Simple of these irregular verbs.

get	→	got	do	→	
buy	→		go	→	
have	→		see	→	

Telling stories

4 🎧 Complete the sentences with Past Simple verbs from this page.

Yesterday I (1) __played__ tennis with Tom. Then
I (2) _____ shopping in town. In a clothes shop
I (3) _____ a lovely jumper. It wasn't expensive,
so I (4) _____ it. Then it (5) _____ to rain,
so I (6) _____ home.

When Annie was young, she (7) __lived__ in a
house near her aunt. Every Sunday she (8) _____
her aunt and (9) _____ tea with her. They
(10) _____ to the radio or (11) _____
TV. Annie loved visiting her aunt because they always
(12) _____ a good time together.

Kevin's week

5 Read about Kevin's week.

Monday

I got up at 9.00 today, so I was late for work. My boss wasn't happy.

I was on Facebook all day. I chatted to my friends. I saw all their photos. I went home at 6 o'clock and watched TV.

Tuesday

I was late for work again. My boss was VERY unhappy.

I went on the Internet and bought some clothes.

In the evening I went to the cinema, but I didn't like the film.

Wednesday

I was late for work AGAIN. My boss said my work wasn't very good.

At lunchtime I went to the pub with some friends. I didn't go back to work in the afternoon. In the evening I saw my girlfriend and we had a pizza.

Thursday

Oh, dear! Late for work again. I played computer games all day. In the evening I went to a party, but I didn't know anybody.

Friday

Late again. My boss said he wanted to talk to me. I went into his office. He said I didn't have a job any more! I said I didn't understand. Everyone at work likes me! Oh, well!

Questions and negatives

6 🎧 Complete the questions about Kevin's week.

1 What time _did he get up_ on Monday morning?
He got up at 9 o'clock.

2 What _____ on Monday evening?
He stayed at home and watched TV.

3 What _____ on the Internet?
He bought some clothes.

4 Where _____ on Tuesday evening?
He went to the cinema.

5 Who _____ on Wednesday?
He saw his girlfriend.

7 Ask and answer the *Yes/No* questions about Kevin.

1 work hard last week?
Did he work hard last week ?
No, he didn't.

2 like the film?
_____ ?
_____

3 have a pizza?
_____ ?
_____

4 enjoy the party?
_____ ?
_____

8 Complete the negative sentences about Kevin.

1 He _didn't get up_ early.

2 He _____ any work all week.

3 He _____ the film.

4 He _____ back to work on Wednesday afternoon.

5 He _____ anybody at the party.

Making conversation

Was it a good match?

9 🎧 Complete the conversations with a question from the box.

~~Was it a good match?~~
Was it good?
What was the score?
What did you do?
Did you buy anything?
What did she cook?
Where did you go?
Is it clean now?

1 **A** I watched the football on TV last night.
   B Oh, did you? **Was it a good match**?
   A Yes, it was great. Arsenal played really well.
   B _____?
   A Arsenal won 2–1.

2 **C** I went to Amy's house for a meal on Sunday.
   D Oh, really? _____?
   C An Italian dish – lasagne.
   D Mmm! _____?
   C It was delicious!

3 **E** I went shopping on Saturday.
   F Did you? _____?
   E That new shopping centre in Hendon.
   F _____?
   E I bought a birthday present for you!
      Happy birthday!

4 **G** I stayed at home all weekend!
   H Oh, dear! _____?
   G I did the housework. The house was so dirty!
   H Was it? _____?
   G Oh, yes! But it was such a boring weekend!

Time expressions

in/at/on

10 Complete the sentences with a preposition (*in*, *at*, or *on*) or no preposition [–].

1 I went to a party __on__ Saturday night.

2 I got up late __–__ yesterday.

3 We went to Spain _____ 2005.

4 I start work _____ 9.00.

5 I phoned you _____ five minutes ago.

6 What did you do _____ last night?

7 I relax _____ the weekend.

8 I started going out with Alice _____ six months ago.

9 We saw James _____ Wednesday.

10 I bought a car _____ last year.

Vocabulary

Sports and leisure activities

11 Look at the pictures and complete the crossword.

go or play?

12 🎧 Complete the sentences with *go* or *play* in the Past Simple and an activity.

 1 Yesterday I **played golf** with my friends.

 2 Last week I _____ in the country.

 3 Ten days ago I _____ in the sea.

 4 At the weekend I _____ for my team.

 5 In 2008 I _____ in the Alps.

 6 I _____ on Saturday. It was a terrible match. 8–0!

 7 Last summer I _____ for the first time. I loved it!

 8 We _____ in the mountains. It was great!

Reading

13 🎧 Read about Daisy's holiday. Use your dictionary.

A holiday in Disneyland

Last year I went on holiday to Disneyland in California. I went with my parents and my sister and brother, and for all of us it was the best holiday!

We stayed in a very big hotel. We were in an apartment. It had four bedrooms and bathrooms, and we had a living room, where there was the biggest TV in the world!

Every day we did something different. One day we went to Universal Studios and saw how they make films.

Another day we went to the Magic Mountain Theme Park and we went on lots of rides. The best was Goliath. Then we went to SeaWorld, where we saw whales and dolphins.

My father was happy because he played golf in the mornings. My mother was happy because she went to the sports club. My sister and brother and I loved it because there was so much to do. Our hotel had three swimming pools! In the evening we went to different restaurants. One night we went to PizzaExpress, where we made our own pizzas! It was great!

And the weather was beautiful all the time we were there.

We had a fabulous time, and we all want to go back!

14 Complete the questions or answers.

1 Where _did Daisy go on holiday_____?
   She went to Disneyland in California.

2 Who did she go with?
   _____ and brother and sister.

3 Where _____?
   In a very big hotel.

4 Did they do the same thing every day?
   No, they _____ every day.

5 What _____ at Universal Studios?
   They saw how they make films.

6 What _____ at the Theme Park?
   They went _____ rides.

7 What did they see at SeaWorld?
   _____.

8 What did her parents do all day?
   Her father _____.
   Her mother _____.

9 Why _____ the children _____ the holiday?
   Because _____ so much to do.

10 What did they do in PizzaExpress?
   _____ their own _____.

Everyday English

Going sightseeing

15 🎧 Write a line from the box to complete the dialogue.

do you want to go	~~a map of the town~~
show me	some information

1 **A** Hello. Can I have _a map of the town_____,
     please?
   B Of course. Here you are.
   A Can you _____ where we
     are on the map?
   B We're here in the city centre.
     Where _____ ?
   A The cathedral. Can you give me
     _____ about it?

does it open	Is it far	is it to get in	does it close

2 **B** Certainly. What do you want to know?
   A _____ from here?
   B Not at all. Just five minutes.
   A What time _____ and what time
     _____ ?
   B It opens at 9.00 and closes at 6.00.
   A And how much _____ ?
   B It's free.

Don't forget!

Grammar

16 Complete the chart.

Past simple

	Positive	Negative	Question
I	played	didn't play	Did I play?
You			Did you play?
He / She	played		
We		didn't play	
They			Did they play?

17 Complete the sentences with *did*, *was*, or *were*.

1 Where _were_ you yesterday at 2.00?
2 I _____ with Henry.
3 What _____ you do yesterday afternoon?
4 _____ you have a good time at the party?
5 I _____ very happy as a child.

18 Write the correct answer.

1 I __went____ to Spain for my last holiday.
   a **goed**   b **went**

2 We _____ with my aunt and uncle.
   a **stayed**   b **staid**

3 I _____ a pair of jeans at the shops.
   a **buyed**   b **bought**

4 _____ them in *Topshop*?
   a **Did you buy**   b **Did you buyed**

5 What _____ last night?
   a **did you**   b **did you do**

6 When _____ to America?
   a **did you go**   b **you go**

did **went**
liked
started
listened

11

can/can't • Adverbs – *very well/not at all*...
• **Requests and offers** • **Adjective + noun**
• **Everyday problems**

I can do that!

can/can't

cook/run fast

1 🎧 Write what the people can do.
Choose from the box.

ride a motorbike	~~cook~~	walk
run fast	sing	play the guitar
ride a horse	ski	speak Russian

1 Laura _can cook._ _____

2 Ben _____

3 Sam _____

4 Anna _____

5 Kirsty _____

6 Andy _____

7 Zoë _____

8 Tony _____

9 Dmitri _____

до свидания

2 Match a line in **A** with a line in **B** and a line in **C**.

A	B	C
A farmer	can fly	a tractor.
An interpreter	can drive	buildings.
A pilot	can cook	several languages.
An architect	can speak	software.
A chef	can write	delicious food.
A computer programmer	can draw	a plane.

Questions and short answers

3 🎧 Ask Mike questions and answer them.

1 **A** <u>Can you play the piano, Mike</u> ?

  M <u>Yes, I can.</u>

2 **A** Can you _____?

  M No, _____

3 **A** _____?

  M _____

4 **A** _____?

  M _____

5 **A** _____ play chess?

  M _____

Negatives

4 🎧 Write negative sentences.

1 Mike / Japanese
  Mike can't speak Japanese. _____

2 Sam / run

  _____

3 You / snowboard

  _____

4 I / write English

  _____

5 We / sing

  _____

6 They / play the piano

  _____

Pronunciation

/kən/ and /kaːnt/

5 🎧 Notice the difference in stress when the sentence is positive or negative.

Positive	I can dance.	can /kən/
Negative	I can't sing.	can't /kaːnt/

🎧 Listen and <u>underline</u> what you hear, *can* or *can't*.

1 I *can* / *can't* play the guitar a little bit.

2 My sister *can* / *can't* cook at all.

3 We *can* / *can't* speak English quite well.

4 I *can* / *can't* understand a word she says.

5 I *can* / *can't* see you on Thursday. Sorry. I'm busy.

6 Peter *can* / *can't* dance really well.

7 We *can* / *can't* go shopping. We don't have any money.

8 You *can* / *can't* all come to my house.

Adverbs

very well/not at all

6 🎧 Listen to Helen. Complete her sentences with words from the box.

very well	really well	~~quite well~~	a little bit	(not) at all	fluently

1 I can speak French _quite well_.
2 My parents can speak Russian _____.
3 I can use a PC _____.

4 I can't use an Apple Mac _____.
5 My sister and I can play tennis _____.
6 But we can ski _____.

Requests and offers

Can I . . . ? Can you . . . ?

7 Complete **A**'s questions with *Can I / you ...?* with a line from the box.

> open the door for me
> ~~have a coffee~~
> give me the salt and pepper
> turn your music down

8 🎧 Complete the dialogues with **B**'s answer from the box.

1 **A** Can I have a coffee, please?
  B _Sure! To have here or take away?_

> ~~Sure! To have here or take away?~~
> I'm sorry. I didn't know it was so loud.
> Of course! Here you are!
> With pleasure! Do you want me to carry something for you?

A Can I _have a coffee_, please?
B _____

A Can you _____, please?
B _____

A Can you _____, please?
B _____

A Can you _____, please?
B _____

Reading

9 🎧 Read the newspaper article.

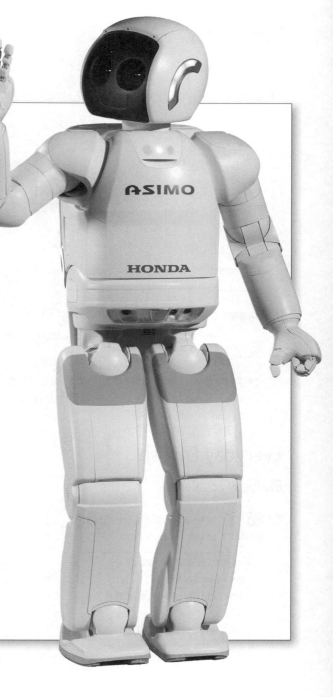

Meet ASIMO, the humanoid robot

Say hello to **ASIMO**, the robot from Honda. He can walk and play football. He can go up and down stairs, and give people drinks.

He can also stand on one foot, dance, and run.

ASIMO stands for 'Advanced Step in Innovative Mobility'.

ASIMO is a people-friendly robot. Honda hopes that one day it can live with people and help them at work and at home.

ASIMO can recognize people's faces, say hello, and shake hands. He can understand when people talk to him, and answer questions.

In May 2008 **ASIMO** conducted the Detroit Symphony Orchestra. He walked onto the stage and said, 'Hello, everyone. This is a beautiful concert hall.' The orchestra then played, and **ASIMO** conducted. At the end of the performance, he gave a bow. Fortunately the music was short. **ASIMO** batteries only last for 20 minutes.

10 Answer the questions.

1 Put a ✓ or a ✗. Can ASIMO …?

✓ walk	☐ play football	☐ drink
☐ sing	☐ dance	☐ run
☐ see	☐ ask questions	☐ speak

2 Who makes ASIMO? _____

3 What does Honda want ASIMO to do? _____

4 Can ASIMO understand when people speak to him? _____

5 What did ASIMO do in May 2008? _____

6 What did ASIMO say? _____

Vocabulary

Adjective + noun

11 Look at the pictures and clues. Do the crossword.

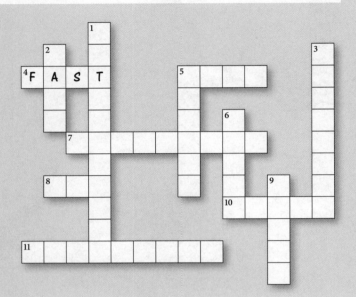

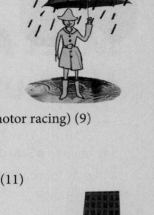

ACROSS

4 a **f _ _ t** car (4)

5 a **b _ _ y** street (not quiet) (4)

7 a **d _ l _ c _ _ _ _ s** meal (9)

8 **w _ _** weather (3)

10 a **y _ _ _ g** man (not old) (5)

11 a **d _ _ g _ r _ _ s** sport (like motor racing) (9)

DOWN

1 an **i _ t _ _ _ _ t _ _ g** book (11)

2 a **t _ _ l** building (4)

3 an **e x c _ _ _ _ g** film (8)

5 a **b _ r _ _ g** lesson (6)

6 a **f _ n _ y** story (5)

9 a **s _ n _ y** morning (5)

Everyday English

Everyday problems

12 🎧 Write the problem in the box under the correct picture.

> This printer doesn't work!
> ~~I can't turn on the TV!~~
> I can't find my plane tickets!
> I'm lost.
> I don't understand what it says.

1 **A** <u>I can't turn on the TV!</u>
   B Push this button.

2 **A** Excuse me! _____
      Where's the town centre?
   B Go straight down here.

3 **A** _____
   B I know. It broke down
      yesterday.

4 **A** _____
   B Give it to me. Maybe I can do
      it for you.

5 **A** Oh, no! _____
   B Calm down! They're in your
      pocket!

Don't forget!

can

13 Complete the chart.

Can	Positive	Question	Negative
I	*I can sing.*	*Can I sing?*	
You			*You can't sing.*
She			
They		*Can they sing?*	

Adverbs

14 Complete the sentences with an adverb from the box.

~~always~~   never   sometimes   often

1 I __always__ check my emails in the evening. (✓✓✓✓)

2 I _____ get up early at the weekend. (✗✗✗✗)

3 I _____ go out with my friends on Saturday night. (✓✓✓✗✓)

4 We _____ go dancing all night. (✗✗✓✗✓)

Regular adverbs end in *-ly*. Complete the sentences with a regular adverb from the box.

~~fluently~~   slowly   usually   carefully

5 Our teacher speaks English __fluently__.

6 I _____ get up at 7.00.

7 I can't understand you. Please speak _____.

8 Do your homework _____. You make a lot of mistakes.

Vocabulary

15 Match the opposite adjectives.

A	B
1 old	a ☐ small
2 good	b ☐ 1 young
3 cheap	c ☐ cold
4 hot	d ☐ bad
5 big	e ☐ expensive
6 old	f ☐ boring
7 fast	g ☐ new
8 dangerous	h ☐ quiet
9 interesting	i ☐ slow
10 busy	j ☐ safe

Prepositions

16 Complete the sentences with a preposition from the box.

with   at   to   for   about   on   of   in

1 I use a computer __at__ work and __at__ home.

2 It's very kind _____ you to invite me _____ your party.

3 I like listening _____ music.

4 I buy clothes _____ the Internet.

5 I play chess _____ a partner _____ Moscow.

6 I chat _____ my friends _____ Facebook.

7 I need some information _____ train times.

8 This is a present _____ you.

9 There's something wrong _____ my computer.

10 Do you want to go _____ a walk?

can't cook at all

can sing well

speak English fluently

12

What's in the basket?

1 Tick (✔) what you can see in the shopping basket.

✔ fruit	☐ water
☐ milk	☐ wine
☐ bread	☐ cheese
☐ meat	☐ cake

some/any

Adam's shop

2 🎧 Look at Adam's shop.
What does/doesn't he have? What is there/isn't there?
He has some ham.   *He doesn't have any cheese.*
There's some ham.   *There isn't any cheese.*

1 He has __some__ orange juice.

2 There isn't __any__ apple juice.

3 There _____ tea.

4 He _____ coffee.

5 He _____ milk.

6 There _____ bread.

7 He _____ fruit.

8 There _____ cake.

Questions

3 Complete the questions and answers.

1 Does Adam have __any__ ham?
   __Yes, he does.__

2 Is there __any__ cheese?
   __No, there isn't.__

3 Does _____ coffee?
   _____

4 Is _____ fruit?
   _____

I'd like

I'd like a… /I'd like to…

4 🎧 Complete the sentences with *I'd like* …

1 I'd like <u>three oranges</u>,
please.

2 I'd like <u>to try on this jumper</u>,
please.

3 I'd like _____,
please.

4 I'd like _____,
please.

5 _____,
please.

6 _____,
please.

Offering things

What would you like?

5 🎧 Complete the questions with *would like* …?

1 **A** What <u>would you like to drink</u> ?

   B I don't know.

   A <u>Would you like a glass of wine</u> ?

   B Er … I don't like wine.

   A Would _____?

   B Ugh, no! I don't drink beer!

   A _____?

   B Yeah, a Coke would be great! Thanks.

2 **A** What <u>would you like to do tonight</u> ?

   B I don't know.

   A Would you like to _____?

   B No. I don't feel like going to the cinema.

   A Would _____?

   B No. I'm not hungry!

   A _____?

   B Now that's a great idea! I'd love to stay home
and watch TV! Maybe we can have a pizza!

like and *would like*

like dancing/would like to dance

6 Tick (✓) the correct sentence.

1 ☑ I love ice cream.
   ☐ I'd love an ice cream

2 ☐ Do you like dancing?
   ☐ Would you like to dance?

3 ☐ Do you like wine?
   ☐ Would you like some wine?

4 ☐ I love shopping!
   ☐ I'd love to go shopping.

5 ☐ I like drinking water.
   ☐ I'd like a drink of water.

6 ☐ Do you like cooking?
   ☐ Would you like to cook?

7 🎧 Read the conversation. <u>Underline</u> the correct forms.

A It's your birthday next week, isn't it? How old are you?

B Don't ask! Too old!

A What (1) <u>*would you like*</u> / *do you like* for your birthday?
   (2) *I like* / *I'd like* to buy you a present! Something nice!

B Well, that's very kind.

A What sort of things are you interested in? What (3) *do you like* / *would you like* doing?

B Well, one of my big passions is reading. (4) *I love* / *I'd love* reading.

A And you (5) *like* / *would like* cooking, don't you?

B Yes, it's true. I (6) *love* / *'d love* cooking.

A Right! That's easy! I'll buy you a cook book! Then you can read and cook!

B That would be lovely! Thank you!

Pronunciation

/e/ /iː/ /uː/ /ɪ/

8 🎧 Write the words about food and drink in the box in the correct column.

bread	chips	cheese	juice
biscuit	breakfast	food	fruit
beans	meal	chicken	meat

/e/	/iː/	/uː/	/ɪ/
egg	cream	soup	fish

Listen and repeat.

9 🎧 Match the words that rhyme.

1 chip   **make**
2 cheap   **my**
3 steak   **please**
4 soup   **sleep**
5 food   **would**
6 cheese   **ship**
7 good   **rude**
8 pie   **group**

Vocabulary

Food

10 Look at the pictures and complete the crossword.

ACROSS

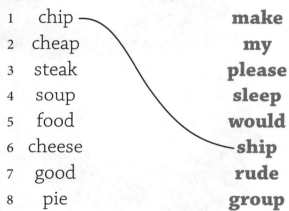

DOWN

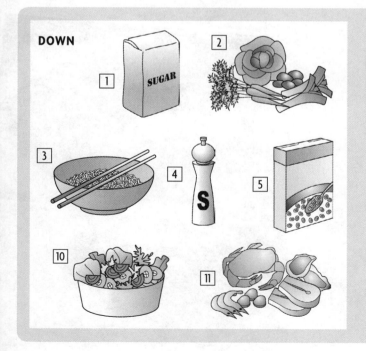

Crossword grid:

4 across: S O U P

Reading

English food

11 🎧 Read the article about English food. Put a tick (✓) if the sentence is true. Put a (✗) if the sentence is false.

1 ☑ People think that English food isn't good.
2 ☒ People know what English food is.
3 ☐ English food is much better now.
4 ☐ English cooks travel to other countries.
5 ☐ Most English people eat a big breakfast.

6 ☐ Lunch is the main meal of the day.
7 ☐ English people eat dinner late.
8 ☐ Sunday lunch is a family meal.
9 ☐ Every town in Britain has international restaurants.
10 ☐ There is good food and bad food in Britain.

What do English people eat?

A REPORT BY JAMES BRADFORD

ENGLISH FOOD has a bad reputation. Everybody knows what French food is, and Italian food, and Chinese food. But what is English food?

It is true that, for many years, food in Britain wasn't good. But it is now possible to eat in England and enjoy it! English cooks know a lot more about how to cook, and they borrow ideas from all over the world.

Breakfast For breakfast, most people have just cereal and maybe toast and jam.
A Full English breakfast is big – sausages, bacon, eggs, tomatoes.

Lunch For many people, lunch is a quick meal at about 1.00 p.m. It isn't a time to relax, because we're too busy at work or at school. So lunch is just a sandwich or a snack.

Dinner The evening meal is our main meal. We don't eat late – we eat at about 8p.m. People have maybe meat or pasta, with vegetables or salad.

Sunday lunch is traditionally the one time in the week when the family eats together.

There is roast meat, such as beef or chicken, with lots of vegetables.

Eating out Every high street in Britain has an Indian restaurant and a Chinese restaurant. In London there are restaurants from all over the world – Greek, Italian, Moroccan, Mexican, Russian, Iranian ... everywhere. Our traditional fast food is fish and chips, and of course there are places to buy hamburgers and pizza.

It is possible to eat really bad food in England. But it is also possible to eat very well!

Don't forget!

Grammar

12 Complete the chart.

I	'd like
You	
He/She	
We	'd like
They	

like / would like / some

13 Write the correct answer.

1 **A** Good morning! Can I help you?
   B Yes. _I'd like_____ some ham, please.

   a **I'd like**   b **I like**

2 **A** Is your teacher nice?
   B Yes. _____ her very much.

   a **I like**   b **I'd like**

3 **A** _____ learning English?
   B Yes, I do. It's interesting.

   a **Would you like**   b **Do you like**

4 **A** I'm thirsty!
   B What _____ to drink?

   a **do you like**   b **would you like**

5 **A** What can I get you?
   B I'd like _____, please.

   a **a Coke**   b **Coke**

6 **A** Who's next? Yes, Madam!
   B I'd like _____, please.

   a **some apples**   b **apples**

Vocabulary

14 Match a shop in **A** with things to buy in **B**.

A	B
1 a chemist's	a ☐ a cheese sandwich
2 a newsagent's	b ☑ some shampoo
3 a post office	c ☐ a kilo of tomatoes
4 a café	d ☐ a pair of jeans
5 a market	e ☐ a pint of beer
6 a railway station	f ☐ some stamps
7 a clothes shop	g ☐ a magazine
8 a pub	h ☐ a return to Manchester

Word order

15 Write the word on the right in the correct place in the sentence.

1 I'd like ^a glass of wine, please.   **a**

2 Would you like cake?   **some**

3 We don't have cheese.   **any**

4 What would you like drink?   **to**

5 Can I have stamps, please?   **some**

6 'James, you like cooking?' 'No, I don't.'   **do**

7 Here are your apples. Do you want else?   **anything**

Would you like...?

I'd like some...

Do you like...?

13

Colours and clothes • Present Continuous
• Present Simple or Continuous
• Opposite verbs – *leave/arrive* • What's the matter?

Here and now

Colours and clothes

1 What colour are these things?

1 a London bus
   red

2 a New York taxi
   yellow

3 milk
   _____

4 the sea
   _____

5 grass
   _____

6 the night
   _____

7 chocolate
   _____

8 clouds
   _____

black   blue
red   brown
green   yellow
grey   white

2 Look at the pictures and complete the crossword.

```
 1            2        3           4
[S][U][I][T] [ ][ ]   [ ][ ][ ]   [ ]
         5 [ ][ ][ ][ ]           [ ]
           [ ]         [ ]        [ ]
                              6   [ ]
         7 [ ]                [ ] [ ]
 8 [ ][ ][ ]   9 [ ][ ][ ][ ]    10[ ]
                                  [ ]
11[ ] 12[ ][ ][ ][ ][ ]           [ ]
[ ]                               [ ]
[ ]                               [ ]
13[ ][ ][ ][ ]
[ ]
```

DOWN

1
2
3
4
6
7
10
11

ACROSS

1
3
5
8
9
12
13

Present Continuous

She's wearing/talking

3 Complete the sentences. What are the people wearing? What are they doing?

1 Anna's wearing <u>a jacket and top</u>.
She's <u>talking on the phone</u>.

2 Paul's wearing _____.
_____ sitting in a café.

3 The kids are _____
and T-shirts.
_____ for a bus.

4 I'm _____ my pyjamas.
I'm _____ a book.

5 We _____ school uniform.
We _____ studying in class.

6 Fay _____ jeans.
_____ an email.

Questions

4 🎧 Complete the questions and answers about the people in exercise 3.

1 Who's <u>Anna talking</u> to?
She's <u>talking</u> to her boyfriend.

2 What's _____?
He's _____ a coffee.

3 Where _____ going?
_____ to school.

4 What _____ you _____?
I _____ *A History of Europe.*

5 What _____ studying?
We _____ physics.

6 Who _____ to?
She _____ friends on Facebook.

Negatives

5 🎧 Look at the two pictures. Write what *isn't* happening in picture **B**.

In picture **B** …

1 the man _isn't wearing a jacket._

2 the children _____

3 the woman _____

4 the dog _____

5 the boys _____

6 the sun _____

7 the ducks _____

8 the boy and girl _____

Present Simple or Continuous?

wear/are wearing

6 🎧 Write the verb in **bold** in the Present Simple or the Present Continuous.

wear

1 Police officers and firemen _wear_____ a uniform.

2 What's that perfume _you're wearing_? It's lovely!

live

3 The President _____ in the White House.

4 I _____ with an English family while I'm in London.

have

5 You can't speak to Pete. He _____ a shower.

6 I _____ three sisters.

speak

7 Our teacher _____ English fluently.

8 That's Olga over there! She _____ to Hans.

(not) work

9 My father _____ any more. He's retired.

10 I'm on holiday this week, so I _____.

(not) rain

11 It _____ much in the Sahara.

12 It _____. We can go out now.

Reading

Today's different

7 🎧 Read about Isabel and Mark. Answer the questions.

Today is different!

Isabel

"On Saturday mornings I usually get up late and do the housework. Then I meet some friends in town for lunch, and go shopping in the afternoon. In the evening I go to the cinema, or go to a party."

But this Saturday is different!
Today Isabel is getting married. She got up early and put on her wedding dress. Now she's in church with all her family and friends. She's wearing a white dress, and her new husband is standing next to her.

Mark

"On Christmas Day we usually all go to my parents' house. We open our presents, then have a big lunch at about 2.00. After that we play games and watch TV."

But this Christmas is different!
Mark and his wife, Donna, are in Australia, and it's summer. They're having Christmas with Donna's parents, who are Australian. This morning they went swimming, and now they're having a barbecue and cooking lunch on the beach. It's hot, and they're wearing shorts.

1 What does Isabel usually do on Saturdays?
2 What is special about today?
3 Where is she?
4 What did she do this morning?
5 What is she wearing?

6 What does Mark usually do on Christmas Day?
7 Where is he today? Why?
8 What did they do this morning?
9 What are they doing now?
10 What are they wearing?

Vocabulary

Opposite verbs

8 🎧 Complete the sentences with the opposite verb in the correct form.

1 **A** Hi, Dave! Are you **leaving** the party already?
  B Actually, *I'm just arriving!*

2 **A** Why are you **selling** your house in London?
  B Because we're _____ a house in the country.

3 **A** I **love** Italians. They're so passionate!
  B I love them, too. But I _____ pasta!

4 **A** Can we **go** now? I'm bored.
  B No! I want _____! It's really interesting!

5 **A** Can I **ask** a question?
  B Sure. But I'm not sure if I can _____ it.

6 **A** Hi, Ben! Do you want to **play** golf today?
  B Sorry! I'm _____. Another day.

7 **A** What time do you **start** work?
  B 9 o' clock.
  A And what time _____ you _____?
  B 5.30 in the afternoon.

8 **A** What's the score?
  B 3–1.
  A Are we **winning**?
  B No, we're _____

9 **A** Excuse me! Can you **open** the door for me?
  B With pleasure!
  A That's very kind. And can you _____ it after me?
  B Of course!

10 **A** My computer isn't working.
  B Well, **turn it off**, wait a minute, then _____ it _____ again. That usually works.

Everyday English

What's the matter?

9 Complete the sentences with words from the boxes.

| tired | hungry | ~~thirsty~~ | cold | bored |

1 I'm **thirsty**   2 I'm _____   3 I'm _____   4 I'm _____   5 I'm _____

| hot | worried | angry | a headache | a cold |

6 I'm _____   7 I have _____   8 I'm _____   9 I have _____   10 I'm _____

10 🎧 Match a line in **A** with a line in **B**.

A		B	
1	I'm thirsty.	a	☐ Why don't you take some aspirin?
2	I'm hungry.	b	☐ Why don't you have an early night?
3	I'm cold.	c	☐! Here! Have some water!
4	I have a headache.	d	☐ Well, why don't we go out and have something to eat?
5	I'm tired.	e	☐ Put on my jumper! It's lovely and warm!

A		B	
6	I'm hot.	f	☐ Why don't you go for a swim?
7	I'm bored.	g	☐ With me? Oh, dear! What did I do?
8	I'm angry.	h	☐ Read this book. It's brilliant!
9	I'm worried.	i	☐ Well, take some aspirin and go to bed!
10	I have a cold.	j	☐ What's new? You're always worried!

Don't forget!

Present Continuous

11 Complete the chart.

Present Continuous

	Positive	Question	Negative
I	*I'm working*	*Am I working*	*I'm not working*
You			*You aren't working*
He/She	*She's working*		
It		*Is it working?*	
We			*We aren't working*
They		*Are they working?*	

12 Write the *-ing* form of the verbs.

wear   _wearing_   live   _living_

read   _____   make   _____

work   _____   have   _____

play   _____   sit   _sitting_

enjoy   _____   swim   _____

do   _____   run   _____

13 Complete the sentences with *'m*, *is*, or *are*.

1 Where _are_ you sitting? Can I sit next to you?

2 I _____ studying English.

3 _____ everyone having a good holiday?

4 My parents _____ working in New York at the moment.

5 I _____ not eating because I _____ not hungry.

14 Complete the sentences with *am*, *is*, *are*, *do*, *does*, or *did*.

1 Where _do_ you like going on holiday?

2 _____ you go away last year?

3 What's that book you _____ reading? Is it good?

4 I _____ reading a very good book at the moment.

5 What _____ this word mean – '*tired*'?

6 Oh, dear! It _____ raining, and I don't have an umbrella.

Vocabulary

15 Match a word in A with a word in B.

A		B	
1 wear	a	☐	hard
2 play	b	☐	a cake
3 make	c	☐	your holiday
4 enjoy	d	☑ 1	a suit
5 work	e	☐	by train
6 travel	f	☐	the guitar

A		B	
7 miss	g	☐	road
8 swimming	h	☐	pool
9 married	i	☐	jumper
10 mobile	j	☐	couple
11 busy	k	☐	phone
12 warm	l	☐	your family

a/an and *the*

16 Complete the sentences with *a/an* or *the*.

1 I wear _a_ suit to work.

2 I get to work at 8.00. I like to be _____ first person in _____ office.

3 Would you like _____ ice cream?

4 I'm always tired at _____ end of _____ day.

5 Tim's _____ businessman.

6 **A** What's _____ matter?
   B I have _____ headache.

7 I'm reading _____ lot.

I'm working

What are you doing?

I'm not running

14

Future plans • Grammar revision • Vocabulary revision • Form filling • Social expressions (2)

It's time to go!

Future plans

going to study/work/travel . . .

1   Read about three young people.

SCHOOL'S FINISHED!

It's the end of school for these 17-year-old students. So what are they planning to do with their lives?

Alice Roberts

Alice is going to study medicine at Edinburgh University.

'I'm really looking forward to it,' says Alice. 'I'm going to live with other students on the campus. I really want to be a doctor and work with children.'

Terry Bradshaw

Terry is going to work with his father, who has a company that imports Italian clothes.

'I'm going to spend three months in Italy,' says Terry. 'I'm going to visit our designers, and I also want to learn Italian.'

Melanie Black

Melanie is going to travel abroad for a year. She has relatives in California, so first she's going to visit them.

'In the new year, I'm going to teach English in Japan,' she says. 'After that, I don't really know what I'm going to do.'

2   Complete the sentences with a name.

1   __Terry__ is going to work in business.
2   _____ is going to be a doctor.
3   _____ is going to teach a language.
4   _____ is going to learn a language.
5   _____ is going to live with other students.
6   _____ doesn't know what she's going to do later.

3   🎧 Complete the questions and answers.

Alice

1   What is __Alice going to study__ ?
     She __'s going to study__ medicine.

2   Where _____?
     She _____ at Edinburgh University.

3   Where _____ to live?
     She _____ on the campus.

Terry

4   Who __is Terry going to work__ with?
     He _____ with his father.

5   How long _____ in Italy?
     He _____ three months there.

6   Who _____ in Italy?
     He _____ their designers.

Melanie

7   What __'s Melanie going to do__ ?
     She _____ travel abroad for a year.

8   Who _____ visit in California?
     She _____ some relatives.

9   What _____ do in Japan?
     She _____ teach English.

What are you doing tomorrow?

4 🎧 Complete the questions and answers. Use the words in brackets (...).

A Right, Sally. We need to get together. When can we meet? ⬚**1** What _are you doing_ (do) tomorrow?

B Tomorrow ⬚**2** I _____ (work) all day.

And then in the evening ⬚**3** I _____ (go) to the _____.

A Oh, interesting! What ⬚**4** _____ you _____ (go/see)?

B It's a new French film called *Passion*.

A What about Tuesday?

B On Tuesday ⬚**5** I _____ (have) lunch with some girlfriends,

and in the afternoon ⬚**6** we _____ (go) _____.

A All right. Wednesday. How are you for Wednesday?

B On Wednesday morning ⬚**7** I _____ (go) to the _____,

and in the afternoon ⬚**8** I _____ (play) tennis.

A Thursday?

B On Thursday ⬚**9** I _____ (see) Henry for coffee,

and in the evening some friends ⬚**10** _____ (come) for dinner.

So on Thursday afternoon ⬚**11** I _____ (cook).

A Oh, very nice. What ⬚**12** _____ you _____ (go/cook)?
B Tomato soup and roast chicken.
A OK! Stop! It's too difficult to find a time when you're free.

Grammar revision

All tenses

5 🎧 Write the verb in brackets in the correct tense.

Our School

Our school (1) **has**_____ (have) one hundred students,
and twenty teachers (2) _____ (work) here.
The school (3) _____ (open) ten years ago,
and I (4) _____ (think) it is one of the best in our town.

Our teacher is lovely. She (5) _____
(come) from a town not far from here. She
(6) _____ (start) working here last year,
and all the students (7) _____ (love)
her. She (8) _____ (help) us all the time,
but she (9) _____ (give) us too much
homework!

Now we (10) _____ (sit) in class doing this exercise. It's a lovely day
– it (11) _____ (not rain). After the lesson I (12) _____ (have)
a coffee with my best friend, Simone.

The course (13) _____ (begin) nine months ago. At first English
(14) _____ (be) very difficult, but now it's OK. We speak a lot better
now! We (15) _____ all _____ (continue) learning English
next year! We enjoy it so much!

Irregular verbs

6 Complete the irregular verbs.

Present	Past		Present	Past
1 come →	came		6 ←	took
2 buy →			7 say →	
3 go →			8 ←	found
4 ←	saw		9 do →	
5 have →			10 make →	

Vocabulary revision

Lists – *Monday/Tuesday . . .*

7 Complete the lists.

1	2	3	4	5	6
Monday	morning	spring	breakfast	always	get up
Tuesday					get dressed
		autumn		sometimes	
	night				
Friday					
					go to bed

7	8
January	ten
	twenty
March	
May	fifty
July	
September	eighty
	a hundred
November	

Words that go together – *tired/work hard*

8 🎧 Match a line in **A** with a line in **B**.

1

A	B
1 I'm tired	a ☐ with my friends.
2 Last night I went out	b ☐ 1 because I work so hard.
3 This morning I had a shower	c ☐ Do you have some aspirin?
4 I love swimming	d ☐ in the sea.
5 I have a headache.	e ☐ and washed my hair.

2

A	B
1 I buy a lot of clothes	a ☐ to going on holiday.
2 We live in a flat	b ☐ on the Internet.
3 We all went out	c ☐ but usually I lose.
4 I'm looking forward	d ☐ for a meal on my birthday.
5 I love playing golf. Sometimes I win,	e ☐ on the second floor.

3

A	B
1 I have a fridge and a cooker	a ☐ There are buses, trains, and ferries.
2 Big cities are usually busy	b ☐ It's warm and sunny.
3 The weather's lovely today.	c ☐ in my kitchen.
4 You don't need a car in this town.	d ☐ three languages fluently.
5 My sister can speak	e ☐ and noisy.

Form filling

Questions and answers

9 🎧 Read the application form. Complete the questions and answers.

OLYMPIC EMPLOYMENT AGENCY

APPLICATION FORM

Mr / Mrs / Miss / Ms (please circle)

First name	**Jennifer**
Surname	**Kelly**
Address	**35 West End Lane** **London**
Post code	**NW5 7GH**

Contact information

Phone	**07988 677432**
email	**jkelly@hotmail.com**

Personal information

Age	**23**
Nationality	**Irish**

Marital status (please tick)

☑ single   ☐ married   ☐ divorced

Education

School	**Hampstead High School**
University	**Bristol**
Subject	**Politics and Education**

Interests

Languages	**English and Spanish**
Sports	**Tennis and running**

DO NOT WRITE HERE
Card   HOX 4627   Data input NNHG/VCSD/8900

Signature	*Jennifer Kelly*

1 <u>What's your first name</u> _____?
   Jennifer.

2 _____?
   Kelly.

3 Where _____?
   London.

4 _____ address?
   35 West End Lane, London.

5 _____?
   NW5 7GH.

6 What's your phone number?
   _____

7 _____?
   jkelly@hotmail.com

8 _____?
   I'm 23.

9 Where _____?
   Ireland.

10 Are you married?
   _____

11 Where _____ school?
   I went to Hampstead High School.

12 Which _____ to?
   Bristol.

13 _____ study?
   I studied politics and education.

14 _____?
   Two. English and Spanish.

15 _____ you do?
   I play tennis and I go running.

Everyday English

Social expressions (2)

10 🎧 Match a line in **A** with a line in **B**.

A		B	
1	How do I get to the station?	a ☐	ticket to Oxford, please?
2	Excuse me!	b ☐	Can you tell me the time, please?
3	I hope you have a good time	c ☐	to drink?
4	Thanks for all your help.	d ☑ 1	Turn right at the church, and go straight on.
5	Can I have a return	e ☐	at the party.
6	What would you like	f ☐	Thanks. Same to you.
7	I'm sorry I'm late.	g ☐	It was very kind of you.
8	Bye! Have a good weekend!	h ☐	Don't worry. It doesn't matter.

Don't forget!

Question words

11 Match a question word in **A** with an answer in **B**.

A		B	
1	What?	a ☐	Jamie.
2	Where?	b ☑ 1	A pair of jeans.
3	When?	c ☐	Because I was tired.
4	Who?	d ☐	By bus.
5	Why?	e ☐	In Paris.
6	How?	f ☐	In 2006.

A		B	
7	How many?	g ☐	£4.60.
8	How much?	h ☐	Six.
9	How old?	i ☐	Twenty-two.
10	How long?	j ☐	Jazz, hip hop, rock n roll.
11	What sort?	k ☐	Medium.
12	What size?	l ☐	An hour.

Prepositions

12 Write in the correct preposition.

1 Mike's __on__ holiday at the moment.

2 I'm living _____ my brother _____ a few weeks.

3 What would you like _____ your birthday?

4 London is the best city _____ the world.

5 I come _____ school _____ bus.

6 I like listening _____ music.

7 Are you interested _____ the cinema?

8 Can I pay _____ this shirt _____ credit card?

9 We're going _____ Greece _____ Saturday.

10 Annie's married _____ Lee. He works _____ Barclays Bank.

on   in

by   to

with   for

Tapescripts

UNIT 1

Exercise 1

1 Hello. I'm Adam.
2 Hello. My name's Bonnie.
3 Hello. My name's Chris.

Exercise 3

1 **A** Carl, this is Liliana Moretti.
   C Hello, Liliana. My name's Carl Erikson.
   L Hello, Carl. Nice to meet you.
2 **B** Ruby, this is Husain Malouf.
   R Hello, Husain. Nice to meet you.
   H And you.
3 **C** Liliana, this is Ruby. Ruby, this is Liliana.
   L Hello, Ruby. I'm Liliana Moretti.
   R Hello. I'm Ruby Harrison.
   L Nice to meet you.
   R And you.

UNIT 2

Exercise 8

J Hello! What's your name?
S My name's Svana.
J Hi, Svana. I'm Jeff.
S Hello, Jeff.
J How are you, Svana?
S I'm fine, thanks.
J Where are you from, Svana?
S I'm from Oslo.
J Oh! Is that in Sweden?
S No! It's in Norway, of course!
J Oh, yes! Look at that girl! Over there!
S Yes, her name's Ingrid.
J Where's she from?
S She's from Norway, too.
J Is she a friend?
S She's my sister.
J Oh!

Exercise 13

Hi! My name's Sofia. I'm from Berlin, in Germany. I'm married. I'm a teacher. My school is in the centre of town. My students are from the United States. They're all American! All fifteen of them!

Hello! My name's Adam. I'm from Sydney, in Australia. I'm married. I'm a doctor.

My hospital is in the centre of town. It's a fantastic building! The doctors are really good!

Exercise 14

1 She's a teacher.
2 He's a doctor.
3 His name's Adam.
4 Her name's Sofia.
5 He's married.
6 She's married.
7 Her students are from the US.
8 He's from Sydney.

Exercise 17

fifteen	twenty-eight	nineteen	twelve
twenty-one	twenty-five	thirteen	
twenty	twenty-two	twenty-six	

UNIT 3

Exercise 10

Interviewer Hi!
Ella Hello!
I You're Ella, right?
E That's right.
I So … I know your first name's Ella, but what's your surname?
E My surname is Smith.
I Ah! Smith! OK. How old are you, Ella?
E I'm 23.
I 23. And you live in Brooklyn, right? What's your address?
E My address is 209, Park Place, New York, NY 11217.
I … Park Place, New York. And your phone number at work? What's your telephone number at work?
E It's 212-786-5893.
I … 786-5893. And your cell phone? What's your cell phone number?
E It's 917-438-6721.
I … -438-6721. Now, you work in newspapers, but what's your job?
E I'm a journalist.
I Oh, wow! How interesting! And … are you married?
E No, I'm not.
I Thank you, Ella. Thank you very much.
E My pleasure.

UNIT 4

Exercise 5

My wife's name is Kim. Our house is nice, but it isn't very big. It's small. It's in north London. Yeah, it's a small house. My sister, Alice, has a house in our street – it's just two minutes from our house. Our children and her children are at the same school, and that's really nice. Alice has three children and we have two – two children and a dog, Ben. My daughter's name is Penny, and my son's name is Archie. The children's school is near our house, so that's good, but my wife's office is miles from our house – about twenty miles. My job is in the centre of town, that's no problem. We're both happy in our jobs, so that's ok. We aren't rich, but we're happy.

Exercise 12

A Good morning. The British Tourist Authority.
B Hello. Can you give me some information about hotels in London, please?
A Of course. Your name is?
B Alfonso Morelli.
A M O R R …
B No, no! M-O-R-E-double L-I. Just one R.
A Thank you. And what's your email address?
B amorelli@superdada.it.
A I'll email you some information today.
B That's very kind. Thank you very much. Goodbye.
A My pleasure. Goodbye.

UNIT 5

Exercise 3

1 Do you like coke?
   Yes, I do. It's great!
2 Do you like football?
   No I don't. It's terrible!
3 Do you like pizza?
   Yes I do. It's delicious!
4 Do you like skiing?
   Yes I do. It's fantastic!
5 Do you like James Bond films?
   Yes I do. They're exciting!
6 Do you like coffee?
   No I don't. It's awful!

Exercise 8

Int Hi, Gracie. Can I ask you a few questions about your parents?

Gracie Of course. No problem.

I Now, your parents live in Spain, don't they?

G That's right. They have a house in Seville. They don't live in England any more.

I Oh! Very nice! Mmm … do they speak Spanish?

G They speak a little Spanish, yes.

I Oh, interesting! And what do they do in Spain? Do they play golf? Do they go swimming?

G They're both quite old now, so they don't do a lot. They're in a tennis club, so in Spain they play tennis.

I Do they work? Do your parents still work?

G No, they don't. They don't work at all now.

I And you live in England, don't you? Where do you and your husband live?

G We don't live in England. We have a house in Scotland.

I And do your mother and father come to visit?

G Oh, yes! My parents come to our house in summer.

I And … do they play tennis in Scotland?

G No. We all play golf together. We love golf!

I Oh, lovely! And do you all go out to restaurants?

G No, not really. We eat at home. I love cooking. So we don't eat in restaurants.

I Well, thank you very much. That's very interesting.

Exercise 16

1 **A** Excuse me! How much is this French–English dictionary?
  B It's £15.75.
  A Thank you.

2 **A** Hi. A cup of coffee, please.
  B To have here or take away?
  A To have here.
  B Small or large?
  A Small. How much is that?
  B £1.55.
  A Thanks.

3 **A** How much are those jeans?
  B The blue ones?
  A Yeah.
  B They're $45.
  A Er … OK.

4 **A** *The Times*, please.
  B 90p.
  A Thanks.

5 **A** Can I help you?
  B Yes. A hamburger, please.
  A Anything to drink?
  B No, just a hamburger.
  A £2.50.
  B Thanks.

6 **A** A strawberry ice-cream, please.
  B There you are, little girl.
  A How much is that?
  B 80p.

7 **A** How much is this orange?
  B Just the one?
  A Yeah, just this orange.
  B Er … 50p.

8 **A** Can I have this CD, please?
  B Sure. That's £13.99, please.
  A Thank you very much.

UNIT 6

Exercise 3

A Excuse me! What time is it?
B It's three-thirty.
A Thank you very much.
B That's OK.

C Excuse me! Do you have the time, please?
D Sure. It's exactly ten o'clock.
C Thanks a lot.
D That's all right.

UNIT 7

Exercise 11

1 **In a café**
  A Can I have a cup of tea, please?
  B Sure. Anything to eat?
  A Yes. Can I have a piece of chocolate cake?
  B Of course. Here you are.
  A How much is that?
  B That's £4.60, please.

2 **In a clothes shop**
  C Do you have this T-shirt in a medium, please?
  D I'll have a look for you.
  C Thanks.
  D Yes. Here you are.
  C Oh! Thank you. Can I try it on, please?
  D Certainly. The changing rooms are over there.

3 **In a train station**
  E Can I have a ticket to Brighton, please?
  F Do you want a single or a return?
  E A single, please.
  F That's £25.50, please.
  E Can I pay by credit card ?
  F Sure. Put your card in the machine. And enter your PIN. Now take your card.

UNIT 8

Exercise 11

1 Go down the High Street. Turn right into Riverside. It's on the right, next to the supermarket.

2 Go down the High Street. It's on the right, next to the post office, on the corner of School Lane.

3 Go straight on down the High Street. It's on the left, next to the Park Hotel.

4 Go down the High Street. Turn left into Albion Street. It's on the left, near the bridge.

5 Go straight on down the High Street. Turn right into School Lane. It's on the right.

Exercise 12

1 **A** Excuse me! Is there a bank near here?
  B Yes. Go straight on. It's on the left, next to the chemist's.
  A Thanks a lot.

2 **C** Excuse me! How do I get to the railway station?
  D Go down the High Street. Turn left. Go down Albion Road. It's near the bridge, on the left.
  C That's very kind. Thank you.

3 **E** Excuse me! How do I get to the sports centre?
  F Go down the High Street. Go past the post office, past School Lane. It's on the right, next to the cinema.
  E Thank you very much.

4 **G** Excuse me! Is there a supermarket near here?
  H Yes. Turn right into Riverside. It's on the right next to the theatre, near the river.
  G Thanks. Bye!

UNIT 9

Exercise 1

1 two thousand and six
2 two thousand
3 two thousand and ten (twenty ten)
4 two thousand and fifteen (twenty fifteen)
5 two thousand and twenty (twenty twenty)
6 nineteen ninety-five
7 nineteen ninety
8 nineteen eighty-two
9 nineteen sixty
10 nineteen sixteen

Exercise 2

1 2009
2 2002
3 2012
4 1999
5 1987
6 1960

Exercise 5

1 My mother was born in Chicago in 1960.
2 My father was born in New York in 1958.
3 I was born in 1985.

4 My grandparents weren't born in the United States.
5 My mother's parents were born in Sweden.
6 My father's parents were born in Ireland.

Exercise 6

1 My mother is a pharmacist.
2 My father is a professor.
3 They were at university together.
4 My father's parents were very poor.
5 My mother's parents weren't married in Sweden. They met in the States.
6 Grandpa Fredrik was an engineer.
7 Grandma Smilla was a piano teacher.
8 Pat and Paddy weren't happy at first. Life was very hard for them.

Exercise 15

1 18th April
2 2nd June
3 3rd September
4 15th January
5 10th May
6 25th December

UNIT 10

Exercise 9

1 A I watched the football on TV last night.
  B Oh, did you? Was it a good match?
  A Yes, it was great. Arsenal played really well.
  B What was the score?
  A Arsenal won 2–1.

2 C I went to Amy's house for a meal on Sunday.
  D Oh, really? What did she cook?
  C An Italian dish – lasagne.
  D Mmm! Was it good?
  C It was delicious!

3 E I went shopping on Saturday.
  F Did you? Where did you go?
  E That new shopping centre in Hendon.
  F Did you buy anything?
  E I bought a birthday present for you! Happy birthday!

4 G I stayed at home all weekend!
  H Oh, dear! What did you do?
  G I did the housework. The house was so dirty!
  H Was it? Is it clean now?
  G Oh, yes! But it was such a boring weekend!

Exercise 15

1 A Hello. Can I have a map of the town, please?
  B Of course. Here you are.
  A Can you show me where we are on the map?

B We're here in the city centre. Where do you want to go?
  A The cathedral. Can you give me some information about it?

2 B Certainly. What do you want to know?
  A Is it far from here?
  B Not at all. Just five minutes.
  A What time does it open and what time does it close ?
  B It opens at 9.00 and closes at 6.00.
  A And how much is it to get in?
  B It's free.

UNIT 11

Exercise 3

1 Can you play the piano, Mike?
  Yes, I can.
2 Can you ride a horse?
  No, I can't.
3 Can you speak Spanish?
  Yes, I can.
4 Can you dance?
  Yes, I can.
5 Can you play chess?
  No I can't.

Exercise 5

1 I can play the guitar a little bit.
2 My sister can't cook at all.
3 We can speak English quite well.
4 I can't understand a word she says.
5 I can't see you on Thursday. Sorry. I'm busy.
6 Peter can dance really well.
7 We can't go shopping. We don't have any money.
8 You can all come to my house.

Exercise 6

1 I can speak French quite well.
2 My parents can speak Russian fluently.
3 I can use a PC really well.
4 I can't use an Apple Mac at all.
5 My sister and I can play tennis quite well.
6 But we can ski really well.

Exercise 8

1 A Can I have a coffee, please?
  B Sure! To have here or take away?

2 A Can you open the door for me, please?
  B With pleasure! Do you want me to carry something for you?

3 A Can you turn your music down, please?
  B I'm sorry. I didn't know it was so loud.

4 A Can you give me the salt and pepper, please?
  B Of course! Here you are!

Exercise 12

1 A I can't turn on the TV!
  B Push this button.

2 A Excuse me! I'm lost. Where's the town centre?
  B Go straight down here.

3 A This printer doesn't work!
  B I know. It broke down yesterday.

4 A I don't understand what it says.
  B Give it to me. Maybe I can do it for you.

5 A Oh, no! I can't find my plane tickets!
  B Calm down! They're in your pocket!

UNIT 12

Exercise 5

1 A What would you like to drink?
  B I don't know.
  A Would you like a glass of wine?
  B Er … I don't like wine.
  A Would you like a glass of beer?
  B Ugh, no! I don't drink beer!
  A Would you like a Coke?
  B Yeah, a Coke would be great! Thanks.

2 A What would you like to do tonight?
  B I don't know.
  A Would you like to go to the cinema?
  B No. I don't feel like going to the cinema.
  A Would you like to go out for dinner?
  B No. I'm not hungry!
  A Would you like to stay home and watch TV?
  B Now that's a great idea! I'd love to stay home and watch TV! Maybe we can have a pizza!

Exercise 7

A It's your birthday next week, isn't it? How old are you?
B Don't ask! Too old!
A What would you like for your birthday? I'd like to buy you a present! Something nice!
B Well, that's very kind.
A What sort of things are you interested in? What do you like doing?
B Well, one of my big passions is reading. I love reading.
A And you like cooking, don't you?
B Yes, it's true. I love cooking.
A Right! That's easy! I'll buy you a cook book! Then you can read and cook!
B That would be lovely! Thank you!

Exercise 9

1 chip   ship
2 cheap   sleep
3 steak   make
4 soup   group
5 food   rude
6 cheese   please
7 good   would
8 pie   my

UNIT 13

Exercise 10

1 **A** I'm thirsty.
   B Here! Have some water!

2 **A** I'm hungry.
   B Well, why don't we go out and have something to eat?

3 **A** I'm cold.
   B Put on my jumper! It's lovely and warm!

4 **A** I have a headache.
   B Why don't you take some aspirin?

5 **A** I'm tired.
   B Why don't you have an early night?

6 **A** I'm hot.
   B Why don't you go for a swim?

7 **A** I'm bored.
   B Read this book. It's brilliant!

8 **A** I'm angry.
   B With me? Oh, dear! What did I do?

9 **A** I'm worried.
   B What's new? You're always worried!

10 **A** I have a cold.
   B Well, take some aspirin and go to bed!

UNIT 14

Exercise 10

1 **A** How do I get to the station?
   B Turn right at the church, and go straight on.

2 Excuse me! Can you tell me the time, please?

3 I hope you have a good time at the party.

4 Thanks for all your help. It was very kind of you.

5 Can I have a return ticket to Oxford, please?

6 What would you like to drink?

7 **A** I'm sorry I'm late.
   B Don't worry. It doesn't matter.

8 **A** Bye! Have a good weekend!
   B Thanks. Same to you.

Answer key

Unit 1

1 See Tapescripts, Exercise 1

2 2 My, your   3 name, My

3 See Tapescripts, Exercise 3

4

First names	Ella, Luke, Robert, Ruby, Alice, Harry, Sophie, Joshua, Catherine
Surnames	McKenna, Bond, Johnson, Blackman

5 1 B Fine thanks
    M I'm OK, thanks
  2 C How are you?
    M very well And you?
  3 R Hi Alice
    A How are you?
    R Very well, thank

6 Across   Down
  1 computer   2 television
  5 hamburger   3 photograph
  8 bag   4 camera
  9 car   6 bus
  10 phone   7 house
  11 sandwich   8 book

7 ten nine four six three one eight five

8 1 9 3 5 10 2 7 6

9 3 one hospital   7 ten students
  4 three buses   8 eight coffees
  5 four pizzas   9 six restaurants
  6 seven teachers 10 nine footballs

10

/s/	/z/	/ɪz/
restaurants students photographs	hotels taxis footballs hospitals pizzas coffees teachers	buses sandwiches houses

11 2 A Goodbye!
    B Goodbye!
  3 A Goodnight!
    B Goodnight!
  4 A Good afternoon!
    B Good afternoon!

12 2 Bye! See you later!
  3 Have a nice day!
  4 A cup of tea, please.
  5 Bye! See you tomorrow!
  6 Sleep well!

13

		Short form
I		I'm
You	are	
It	is	It's

14 2 's   3 are   4 's   5 'm   6 Are   7 's

15 2 a   3 a   4 a   5 a   6 b

16 2 I'm fine, thanks.
  3 And you.
  4 Bye! See you tomorrow!
  5 It's a book.

17 2 My name's Anna.
  3 What's this in English?
  4 It's a computer.
  5 How are you, Mika?
  6 I'm fine, thank you.

Unit 2

1 Across   Down
  7 Spain   1 Australia
  8 England   2 France
  9 Japan   3 United States
  10 Brazil   5 China
  12 Russia   6 Egypt
                11 Italy

2

●	●●	●●	●●●	●●●●	●●●●
Spain France	China Egypt England Russia	Japan Brazil	Hungary Italy	United States	Australia

3

♀	Anna	Tatiana		her
♂	his		Henry	he

4 b His c His d Her

5 b She's c He's d She's

6 2 Her, She's
  3 Her, She's
  4 His, He's
  5 Her, She's
  6 His, He's
  7 Her, She's
  8 His, He's

7 2 d   3 a   4 c

8 See Tapescripts, Exercise 8

9 2 e   3 a   4 f   5 c   6 d

10 good, really good, fantastic, OK, bad, awful

12 1 England, Egypt, Malaysia.
  2 ✗   3 ✓   4 ✗   5 ✓   6 ✓   7 ✗
  8 ✗   9 ✓

Carla and Pedro are in Egypt.
Catherine and Anthony are in Malaysia.
Ann and James are in England.

13 See Tapescripts, Exercise 13

14 2 He's   3 His   4 Her   5 He's
  6 She's   7 Her   8 He's

15 13 thirteen   15 fifteen
  21 twenty-one 30 thirty
  22 twenty-two 25 twenty-five
  19 nineteen   28 twenty-eight
  26 twenty-six 20 twenty
  12 twelve   11 eleven
  16 sixteen

16 eleven   twenty-nine
  eighteen   twenty-four
  fourteen   twenty-seven

17 19 12 21 25 13 20 22 26

18

		Short form
I	am	
You	are	You're
He	is	
She		She's
It	is	It's
They	are	They're

19 1 'm   2 are, 'm   3 are, 're
  4 Is, is, 's   5 are, 's, 's

20 2 b   3 a   4 a   5 b

21 2 photograph 3 cup of tea 4 house
5 camera 6 sandwich 7 book
8 bag

22 3 You're 4 your 5 You're 6 your

Unit 3

1
Across	Down
3 doctor	1 businessman
4 taxi driver	2 police officer
8 nurse	5 student
9 shop assistant	6 builder
10 bus driver	7 teacher

2 1 's 2 isn't, 's 3 isn't, 's

3 First name, Country, Address,
Phone number, Mobile number,
Age, Job, Married

4 2 What's his first name?
3 Where's he from?
4 What's his address?
5 What's his phone number?
6 What's his mobile number?
7 How old is he?
8 What's his job?
9 Is he married?

5 2 He isn't from Australia. He's from
England.
3 His isn't 23. He's 26.
4 He isn't a student. He's an engineer.
5 He isn't married.

6 3 Yes, he is. 4 No, he isn't.
5 No, he isn't. 6 Yes, he is.

7 2 Peter isn't a taxi driver. He's a bus driver.
3 We aren't from Spain. We're from Italy.
4 I'm not married. I'm single.
5 You aren't a nurse. You're a student.
6 Paul and Donny McNab aren't doctors.
They're singers in a band.

8 2 a 3 b 4 b 5 a 6 b

9 2 Is Bo from Sweden?
3 What's his job?
4 Where are they on tour?
5 Is Lisa with the band?

10 See Tapescripts, Exercise 10

11 See Tapescripts, Exercise 10

12 2 interesting 3 band, singers
4 city, town 5 tired 6 different
7 station 8 here 9 understand
10 excited

13 2 I'm sorry.
3 That's all right.
4 Excuse me!
5 I don't understand.
6 I don't know.

14
	Positive	Negative
I	am	
You	are	You aren't
He	is	
She		She isn't
It	is	It isn't
We		We aren't
They	are	They aren't

15 2 b 3 b 4 b 5 b 6 b

16 2 from 3 in 4 of 5 of 6 on
7 of 8 in, of 9 at 10 with

17 12 21 75 50 15 8 42 10 38

18 forty-five seven sixty-eight
one hundred

Unit 4

1 2 Bonny's 3 Nick's 4 Alice's
5 Suzie's 6 Harry's 7 Kate's 8 Sarah's

2 2 Her 3 Our 4 your 5 His 6 Their

3
Across	Down
7 father	1 parents
8 son	2 daughter
9 mother	4 husband
10 wife	5 brother
	6 sister

4 3 She has 4 They have 5 She has
6 He has 7 They have 8 He has
9 She has

5 3 ✓ 4 ✓ 5 ✗ 6 ✗ 7 ✓ 8 ✗
9 ✓ 10 ✗

6 2 his sister's
3 his daughter's
4 his son's
5 his dog's

7 2 has 3 her 4 children's 5 wife's
6 We're

8 3 ✓ 4 ✗ 5 ✓ 6 ✗ 7 ✗ 8 ✓ 9 ✗

9 2 f 3 e 4 c 5 h 6 d 7 a 8 b

10 3 Their
4 They're
5 Their
6 they're

11 1 s c h o o l 5 d a u g h t e r
2 h u s b a n d 6 h o s p i t a l
3 w i f e 7 n u r s e
4 s o n 8 f r i e n d s

12 See Tapescripts, Exercise 12

13 your her our

14 have has have have

15 2 a 3 b 4 a 5 a 6 b

16
Places	People	Things
town	accountant	bag
country	police officer	car
village	sister	bus
apartment	waiter	dictionary

17
Singular	Plural
	schools
	cars
	cities
job	babies
family	addresses
woman	sandwiches
	children
	people

Unit 5

1
Across	Down
4 tennis	1 wine
6 pizza	2 swimming
7 ice cream	3 skiing
9 coffee	4 tea
11 football	5 beer
12 hamburger	8 Coke
	10 orange

2 3 I like beer.
4 I don't like swimming.
5 We like skiing.
6 They like wine.
7 We don't like football.
8 You like ice cream.
9 They don't like Chinese food.

3 See Tapescripts, Exercise 3

4 2 have 3 live 4 have 5 speak
6 swim 7 eat 8 drink 9 like
10 want

5 2 What's your father's job?
3 Where do you live?
4 What do you eat?

6 2 do you have
3 do you drink
4 do you like

7 2 don't drink
3 don't live
4 don't live
5 don't

8 See Tapescripts, Exercise 8

9 2 do, do, Do
3 Do they both
4 do, live
5 do you, go

10 2 don't do
3 They don't
4 don't live
5 we don't eat

11

●●	●●	●●●	●●●	●●●●
English Spanish German	Chinese	Arabic Mexican	Japanese Portuguese	Italian American Brazilian

12 2 American 3 German 4 Japanese
5 Arabic 6 Italian 7 Mexican
8 Chinese 9 Brazilian 10 Spanish

13 48, 35, eighty-one, ninety
15, 72, sixty, fifty-nine one hundred

14 £25.99 twenty-five pounds ninety-nine p
£4.50 four pounds fifty
95p ninety-five p
£32 thirty-two pounds
£79 seventy-nine pounds
£2.15 two pounds fifteen
$65 sixty-five dollars
80€ eighty euros
£1.20 one pound twenty

15 3 forty p 40p
4 eighty-eight pounds £88
5 twelve pounds sixty £12.60
6 seventy-five euros 75€
7 one pound twenty £1.20
8 thirty dollars $30

16 See Tapescripts, Exercise 16

17

	Positive	Question	Negative
I			I don't work
You	You work	Do you work?	
We	We work	Do we work?	We don't work
They	They work		They don't work

18 2 a 3 a 4 b 5 b

19 2 speak 3 work 4 have 5 play
6 come

20 2 a 3 an 4 an 5 a

21 2 We live in a big house in London.
3 I'm a waiter.
4 I work in an Italian restaurant.
5 They have an office in the centre of
town.
6 Jamie is an English teacher.

22 2 I have a small flat.
3 Italian people are nice.
4 I don't like Chinese food.
5 My father has an important job.

1 2 three o'clock 3 eight thirty
4 six forty-five 5 two forty-five
6 twelve o'clock

2 2 7.30 3 three o'clock
4 10.45 5 2.30

3 See Tapescripts, Exercise 3

4 1 7.00 o'clock.
2 do you have
3 do you go
4 do you watch, watch

5 3 He has 4 She leaves 5 He does
6 She watches 7 He lives 8 She works

6 1 has 2 goes 3 has 4 leaves
5 does 6 lives 7 has 8 watches

7 2 does she go
3 does she have
4 does she do
5 does George live
6 does he have
7 does he
8 does he do

8 2 does 3 She loves 4 She likes
5 She likes 6 She likes 7 She loves
8 She loves 9 She reads

9 2 doesn't 3 doesn't 4 don't 5 doesn't

10 2 am 3 Is 4 is 5 Do 6 do
7 is 8 Do 9 do 10 are 11 Does
12 does

11

/z/	/s/	/iz/
lives plays does has listens	eats cooks works	teaches

12 2 on 3 at 4 In 5 on 6 at 7 on
8 No 9 No 10 No

13

Across	Down
6 drink	1 work
7 watch	2 office
8 play	3 listen
9 drive	5 shopping
10 lunch	9 dinner
12 languages	10 live
13 early	11 have

15 2 do they go
3 does Michelle do
4 does he
5 does he
6 does he work

16 2 No, she doesn't.
3 Yes, he does.
4 Yes, they do.

17 2 doesn't 3 don't 4 doesn't have

18 Tuesday Wednesday Thursday Friday
Saturday Sunday

19

Positive	Question	Negative
		I don't work
You work	Do you work?	
He works		He doesn't work
	Does she work?	She doesn't work
It works	Does it work?	

20 3 watches 4 cooks 5 work
6 teaches

21 2 does 3 does 4 Do 5 don't
6 don't

22 2 How 3 How much 4 Where
5 Who 6 When 7 How many

23 2 the
3 –, the, –
4 the
5 –
6 –, –
7 –
8 the
9 the, –
10 the, –

1 Who do you live with?
What does Vanessa do?
How old are your children?
Where do you live?
Why do you live in France?
How many languages do you speak?
Do you play any musical instruments?
What car do you drive?
How much money do you have?

2 2 e 3 f 4 a 5 c 6 d 7 h 8 g
9 i 10 j

3 2 When In the summer.
3 How By bus.
4 Where In a village near the sea.
5 Who Jane.
6 Why Because my wife is French.
7 How old
8 How many Three.
9 What time 6.30 in the morning.
10 How much £5.30.

4 2 How do you spell your surname?
3 What's your mobile number?
4 How old are you?
5 What's your favourite food?
6 Do you live in a house or a flat?

5 2 Why does he drive an old car?
Because he doesn't have any money.

3 Why does she stay at home every day?
Because she works at home.

4 Why does she sit at her computer for ten hours a day?
Because she's a writer.

6

Object	Possessive
him	his
	her
it	
us	our
them	

7 1 you 2 her 3 me 4 it 5 him
6 you 7 you, me 8 us 9 them
10 it

8 2 your 3 His 4 Her 5 its 6 Our
7 their

9 3 that 4 This 5 This 6 that

10 2 lovely 3 hot 4 big 5 delicious
6 beautiful 7 cheap 8 wonderful

1 terrible 2 wet 3 awful 4 old
5 cold 6 expensive 7 small
8 happy

11 See Tapescripts, Exercise 11

12
Across	Down
1 shampoo	2 present
3 clothes	3 credit card
4 shoes	6 chips
5 coat	7 bridge
10 postcards	8 letter
11 buildings	9 stamps

13 2 b 3 a 4 a 5 b 6 b

14 2 in 3 for 4 at 5 to 6 to 7 of
8 for 9 to, for 10 with

Unit 8

1 2 living room 3 kitchen 4 bathroom
5 bedroom

2 2 bed 3 cooker 4 sofa 5 desk
6 table 7 laptop 8 armchair

3 2 magazines
3 a toilet
4 a PlayStation®
5 posters
6 a balcony

4 3 ✗ 4 ✗ 5 ✗ 6 ✓

5 2 There are
3 There's
4 There's
5 There are
6 There's

6 2 There isn't
3 There aren't
4 There isn't
5 There aren't
6 There isn't

7 2 Is there, Yes, there is.
3 Are there, Yes, there are.
4 Are there, No, there aren't.

8 2 under
3 next to
4 in
5 in
6 next to

9
Across	Down
4 rain	1 seafood
5 ferry	2 sunbathe
7 mountains	3 park
9 theatre	6 fishing
11 sailing	8 beach
	10 train

10 2 railway station
3 church
4 park
5 car park
6 sports centre
7 supermarket
8 chemist's

11 1 theatre
2 café
3 the park
4 railway station
5 the school

12 See Tapescripts, Exercise 12

13 3 ✗ There are four trains an hour to London.
4 ✗ It takes 30–40 minutes to get into London from Berkhamsted.
5 ✗ There are several hotels in town.
6 ✓
7 ✓
8 ✓
9 ✗ There isn't a theatre, but there is a cinema.
10 ✗ There are two pubs on the High Street.

14 2 a 3 b 4 a 5 a 6 b 7 b 8 a

15 2 but 3 and 4 but

16 2 because 3 because 4 so

17
	13
8	12
30	58
25	9
60	42

18 four seventy-two eighty-eight ten

Unit 9

1 See Tapescripts, Exercise 1

2 See Tapescripts, Exercise 2

3 2 nineteen forty
3 nineteen ninety-nine
4 nineteen seventy-three
5 two thousand and one
6 two thousand and five
7 two thousand and eight
8 two thousand and twelve – twenty twelve

4 1 1989 2 2004 3 1963 4 1945
5 1969

5 See Tapescripts, Exercise 5

6 See Tapescripts, Exercise 6

7 2 was she born
3 were, born
4 was

8 2 wasn't born
3 weren't born
4 weren't

9 1 He was a painter and filmmaker.
2 In Pittsburg, Pennsylvania.
3 From Slovakia.
4 He was a coal miner.
5 No, he wasn't.
6 He was a painter in advertising and magazines.
7 A centre for artists, musicians, and writers.
8 Doctors and hospitals.

1 In Sandringham, England.
2 John, Earl Spencer and Frances, Viscountess Althorp.
3 The Royal family.
4 No, she wasn't.
5 She was a dance teacher and a teacher in a children's school.
6 20.
7 In Paris.
8 Dodi Al-Fayed.

10 2 was 3 were 4 bought 5 said
6 found 7 thought 8 came 9 saw

11 2 were, saw 3 said 4 were, thought
5 came, found 6 went, bought

12
Across	Down
3 home	1 time
4 walk	3 housework
9 shopping	5 lunch
10 shower	6 breakfast
11 exercise	7 work
	8 homework

13 April, June, August, October, December

14 2nd 3rd 4th 5th 7th 10th
12th 20th 21st

16

Positive	Negative
	wasn't
were	
was	wasn't
	weren't
were	

17 2 a 3 b 4 b 5 a 6 b

18

Present	Past
	had
do	
	saw
	bought
say	
	found
come	
	made

19 3 made 4 made 5 did 6 made

20 2 …to the cinema…
3 I do my…
4 …because it is…
5 …have a shower,…
6 'What do you do?' 'I'm a businessman.'
7 I usually have…

Unit 10

1
watched	lived
wanted	phoned
listened	visited
started	loved
worked	stayed

2

/t/	/d/	/ɪd/
watched worked liked	played listened lived phoned loved stayed	wanted started visited

3 bought had did went saw

4 2 went 3 saw 4 bought 5 started
6 went 8 visited 9 had 10 listened
11 watched 12 had

6 2 did he do 3 did he buy 4 did he go
5 did he see

7 2 Did he like the film? No, he didn't.
3 Did he have a pizza? Yes, he did.
4 Did he enjoy the party? No, he didn't.

8 2 didn't do
3 didn't enjoy
4 didn't go
5 didn't know

9 See Tapescripts, Exercise 9

10 3 in 4 at 5 – 6 – 7 at 8 –
9 on 10 –

11
Across	Down
1 ice skating	2 skiing
4 swimming	3 horse riding
6 tennis	5 windsurfing
8 golf	7 fishing
12 cycling	9 football
13 walking	10 dancing
14 rugby	11 cards
15 sailing	

12 2 went cycling
3 went swimming
4 played rugby
5 went skiing
6 played football
7 went windsurfing
8 went horse riding

14 2 She went with her parents
3 did they stay?
4 didn't do the same thing
5 did they see
6 did they do, on lots of
7 They saw whales and dolphins.
8 played golf, went to the sports club.
9 did the children love, there was
10 They made their own pizzas.

15 See Tapescripts, Exercise 15

16

Positive	Negative	Question
played	didn't play	
	didn't play	Did he/she play?
played		Did we play?
played	didn't play	

17 2 was 3 did 4 Did 5 was

18 2 a 3 b 4 a 5 b 6 a

Unit 11

1 2 can speak Russian.
3 can walk.
4 can ride a horse.
5 can ski.
6 can play the guitar.
7 can run fast.
8 can sing.
9 can ride a motorbike.

2 An interpreter can speak several
languages.
A pilot can fly a plane.
An architect can draw buildings.
A chef can cook delicious food.
A computer programmer can write
software.

3 See Tapescripts, Exercise 3

4 2 Sam can't run.
3 You can't snowboard.
4 I can't write English.
5 We can't sing.
6 They can't play the piano.

5 See Tapescripts, Exercise 5

6 2 fluently 3 really well 4 at all
5 quite well 6 really well

7 & 8 See Tapescripts, Exercise 8

10
✓	✗
play football	drink
dance	sing
run	ask questions
see	
speak	

2 Honda.
3 Honda wants ASIMO to live with
people and help them at work and at
home.
4 Yes, he can.
5 He conducted the Detroit Symphony
Orchestra.
6 He said: 'Hello, everyone. This is a
beautiful concert hall.'

11
Across	Down
4 fast	1 interesting
5 busy	2 tall
7 delicious	3 exciting
8 wet	5 boring
10 young	6 funny
11 dangerous	9 sunny

12 See Tapescripts, Exercise 12

13

Positive	Question	Negative
		I can't sing
You can sing	Can you sing?	
She can sing	Can she sing?	She can't sing
They can sing		They can't sing

14 2 never 3 often 4 sometimes
6 usually 7 slowly 8 carefully

15 2 d 3 e 4 c 5 a 6 g 7 i 8 j
9 f 10 h

16 2 of, to 3 to 4 on 5 with, in
6 with, on 7 about 8 for
9 with 10 for

Unit 12

1 ✓ milk, bread, water, cheese

2 3 is some
4 doesn't have any
5 has some
6 isn't any
7 has some
8 isn't any

3 3 he have any, No, he doesn't.
4 there any, Yes, there is.

4 3 a glass of red wine
4 some shampoo for dry hair
5 I'd like to send this parcel,
6 I'd like to buy this magazine

5 See Tapescripts, Exercise 5

6 2 Would you like to dance?
3 Would you like some wine?
4 I love shopping
5 I'd like a drink of water.
6 Do you like cooking?

7 See Tapescripts, Exercise 7

8

/e/	/iː/	/uː/	/ɪ/
egg bread breakfast	cream cheese beans meal meat	soup juice food fruit	fish chips biscuit chicken

9 See Tapescripts, Exercise 9

10 Across
4 soup
6 chicken
7 apple pie
8 salmon
9 jam
11 sparkling
12 still

Down
1 sugar
2 vegetables
3 rice
4 salt
5 cereal
10 salad
11 seafood

11 3 ✓ 4 ✓ 5 ✗ 6 ✗ 7 ✗ 8 ✓
9 ✓ 10 ✓

12

'd like
'd like
'd like

13 2 a 3 b 4 b 5 a 6 a

14 2 g 3 f 4 a 5 c 6 h 7 d 8 e

15 2 …like some cake…
3 …have any cheese…
4 …like to drink…
5 …have some stamps…
6 'James, do you like…'
7 Do you want anything else?

Unit 13

1 3 white 4 blue 5 green 6 black
7 brown 8 grey

2 Across
1 suit
3 tie
5 boots
8 shorts
9 trainers
12 jumper
13 scarf

Down
1 shoes
2 socks
3 T-shirt
4 jacket
6 shirt
7 trousers
10 skirt
11 dress

3 2 a suit, He's
3 wearing trousers, They're waiting
4 wearing, reading
5 're wearing, 're
6 's wearing, She's writing

4 2 Paul drinking, drinking
3 are they, They're going
4 are you reading? 'm reading
5 are you, 're studying
6 is she writing emails, 's writing to

5 In picture B:
1 the man isn't wearing a jacket.
2 the children aren't eating ice cream.
3 the woman isn't wearing sunglasses.
4 the dog isn't eating a bone.
5 the boys aren't playing football.
6 the sun isn't shining.
7 the ducks aren't swimming on the pond.
8 the boy and girl aren't talking.

6 3 lives 4 'm living 5 's having
6 have 7 speaks 8 's speaking
9 doesn't work 10 'm not working
11 doesn't rain 12 isn't raining

7 1 She usually gets up late and does the housework.
2 She's getting married.
3 She's in church.
4 She got up early and put on her wedding dress.
5 She's wearing a white dress.
6 He usually goes to his parents' house.
7 He's in Australia. They're having Christmas with Donna's parents.
8 They went swimming.
9 They're having a barbecue.
10 They're wearing shorts.

8 2 buying 3 hate 4 to stay 5 answer
6 working 7 do you finish 8 losing
9 close 10 turn it on

9 2 cold 3 bored 4 tired 5 hungry
6 hot 7 a cold 8 worried
9 a headache 10 angry

10 See Tapescripts, Exercise 10

11

Positive	Question	Negative
You're working	Are you working?	
	Is he/she working?	He/She isn't working
It's working		It isn't working
We're working	Are we working?	
They're working		They aren't working

12 reading   making
working   having
playing
enjoying   swimming
doing   running

13 2 'm 3 Is 4 are 5 'm, 'm

14 2 Did 3 are 4 am 5 does 6 is

15 2 f 3 b 4 c 5 a 6 e 7 l 8 h 9 j
10 k 11 g 12 i

16 2 the, the 3 an 4 the, the
5 a 6 the, a 7 a

Unit 14

2 2 Alice 3 Melanie 4 Terry 5 Alice
6 Melanie

3 2 is she going to study?
…'s going to study
3 is she going
…'s going to live
4 's going to work
5 is he going to spend
…'s going to spend
6 is he going to visit
…'s going to visit
7 's going to
8 is she going to
…'s going to visit
9 is she going to
…'s going to

4 2 'm working
3 'm going to the cinema
4 are you going to see?
5 'm having
6 're going shopping.
7 'm going to the dentist
8 'm playing tennis
9 'm seeing
10 are coming
11 'm cooking
12 are you going to cook?

5 2 work 3 opened 4 think 5 comes
6 started 7 love 8 helps 9 gives
10 are sitting 11 isn't raining
12 'm going to have 13 began
14 was 15 are all going to continue

6 2 bought 3 went 4 see 5 had
6 take 7 said 8 find 9 did
10 made

7 1 Wednesday, Thursday, Saturday, Sunday
2 afternoon, evening
3 summer, winter
4 lunch, dinner
5 often, never
6 have breakfast, go to work / school,
come home, have dinner
7 February, April, June, August, October,
December
8 thirty, forty, sixty, seventy, ninety

8 1 2 a 3 e 4 d 5 c
2 1 b 2 e 3 d 4 a 5 c
3 1 c 2 e 3 b 4 a 5 d

9 2 What's your surname?
3 do you live?
4 What's your
5 What's your postcode?
6 07988677432
7 What's your email address?
8 How old are you?
9 were you born?
10 No, I'm single.
11 did you go to
12 university did you go
13 What did you
14 How many languages can you speak?
15 What sports do

10 See Tapescripts, Exercise 10

11 2 e 3 f 4 a 5 c 6 d 7 i 8 g 9 h
10 l 11 j 12 k

12 2 with, for 3 for 4 in 5 to, by 6 to
7 in 8 for, by 9 to, on 12 to, for

Notes

Phonetic symbols

Consonants

1	/p/	as in	**pen**	/pen/
2	/b/	as in	**big**	/bɪg/
3	/t/	as in	**tea**	/tiː/
4	/d/	as in	**do**	/duː/
5	/k/	as in	**cat**	/kæt/
6	/g/	as in	**go**	/gəʊ/
7	/f/	as in	**four**	/fɔː/
8	/v/	as in	**very**	/'veri/
9	/s/	as in	**son**	/sʌn/
10	/z/	as in	**zoo**	/zuː/
11	/l/	as in	**live**	/lɪv/
12	/m/	as in	**my**	/maɪ/
13	/n/	as in	**now**	/naʊ/
14	/h/	as in	**happy**	/'hæpi/
15	/r/	as in	**red**	/red/
16	/j/	as in	**yes**	/jes/
17	/w/	as in	**want**	/wɒnt/
18	/θ/	as in	**thanks**	/θæŋks/
19	/ð/	as in	**the**	/ðə/
20	/ʃ/	as in	**she**	/ʃiː/
21	/ʒ/	as in	**television**	/'telɪvɪʒn/
22	/tʃ/	as in	**child**	/tʃaɪld/
23	/dʒ/	as in	**German**	/'dʒɜːmən/
24	/ŋ/	as in	**English**	/'ɪŋglɪʃ/

Vowels

25	/iː/	as in	**see**	/siː/
26	/ɪ/	as in	**his**	/hɪz/
27	/i/	as in	**twenty**	/'twenti/
28	/e/	as in	**ten**	/ten/
29	/æ/	as in	**bag**	/bæg/
30	/ɑː/	as in	**father**	/'fɑːðə/
31	/ɒ/	as in	**hot**	/hɒt/
32	/ɔː/	as in	**morning**	/'mɔːnɪŋ/
33	/ʊ/	as in	**football**	/'fʊtbɔːl/
34	/uː/	as in	**you**	/juː/
35	/ʌ/	as in	**sun**	/sʌn/
36	/ɜː/	as in	**learn**	/lɜːn/
37	/ə/	as in	**letter**	/'letə/

Diphthongs (two vowels together)

38	/eɪ/	as in	**name**	/neɪm/
39	/əʊ/	as in	**no**	/nəʊ/
40	/aɪ/	as in	**my**	/maɪ/
41	/aʊ/	as in	**how**	/haʊ/
42	/ɔɪ/	as in	**boy**	/bɔɪ/
43	/ɪə/	as in	**hear**	/hɪə/
44	/eə/	as in	**where**	/weə/
45	/ʊə/	as in	**tour**	/tʊə/

OXFORD
UNIVERSITY PRESS

Great Clarendon Street, Oxford OX2 6DP

Oxford University Press is a department of the University of Oxford.
It furthers the University's objective of excellence in research, scholarship,
and education by publishing worldwide in

Oxford New York

Auckland Cape Town Dar es Salaam Hong Kong Karachi
Kuala Lumpur Madrid Melbourne Mexico City Nairobi
New Delhi Shanghai Taipei Toronto

With offices in

Argentina Austria Brazil Chile Czech Republic France Greece
Guatemala Hungary Italy Japan Poland Portugal Singapore
South Korea Switzerland Thailand Turkey Ukraine Vietnam

OXFORD and OXFORD ENGLISH are registered trade marks of
Oxford University Press in the UK and in certain other countries

ISBN: 978 0 19 477117 7

Printed in China

This book is printed on paper from certified and well-managed sources.

ACKNOWLEDGEMENTS

*The publisher would like to thank the following for permission to reproduce
photographs*: Alamy pp.4 (Chris/Jupiter Images/Brand X), 4 (shaking hands
outside/PhotoAlto), 4 (shaking hands in office/Jupiterimages/Creatas), 5
(shaking hands/PhotoAlto), 8 (elderly couple/The Photolibrary Wales), 11
(Karima/Bill Bachmann), 11 (Tatiana/Blaine Harrington III), 13 (Petronas
Towers/Beaconstox), 19 (woman/Form Advertising), 24 (family/Cultura), 25
(couple/NewStock), 34 (checking time/Blend Images), 44 (coffee shop/Chris
Howes/Wild Places Photography), 50 (Berkhamstead Town Hall/Robert
Stainforth), 62 (Disneyland/Arco Images GmbH), 64 (man on motorbike/Chris
Pancewicz), 77 (little boys/Jupiterimages/Comstock Images); Corbis UK Ltd.
pp.4 (men shaking hands/John Henley), 8 (waitress taking order/Radius
Images), 8 (mother kissing daughter goodnight/Somos Images), 11 (Yong/
Justin Guariglia), 13 (Sphynx/Hugh Sitton), 13 (Buckingham Palace/Image
Source), 30 (Michael Phelps/Kay Nietfeld/Epa), 52 (JFK/Bettmann); dkimages.
com pp.44 (ticket counter/Chris Stowers), 63 (looking at tourist brochures/
Tony Souter); Getty Images pp.4 (woman with name tag/George Doyle/
Stockbyte), 4 (businessman/Ciaran Griffin/Stockbyte), 8 (businesswoman
waving/Stockbyte), 11 (Kevin/Yellow Dog Productions) 31 (older couple/James
Darell/Digital Vision), 52 (cyclists/Donald Miralle), 53 (washing dishes/Bert
Hardy/Picture Post/Hulton Archive), 53 (walking on beach/H. Armstrong
Roberts/Retrofile); Honda (UK) p.67 (ASIMO); iStockphoto pp.6 (road sign/
Mustafa Deliormanli), 6 (number 6/Lok Sum Fung), 32 (coffee/Murat Giray
Kaya), 43 (miserable Mike/Rosemarie Gearhart), 43 (happy Annie), 53 (couple
on sofa/Trista Weibell), 58 (reading/Vadim Ponomarenko), 64 (cooking), 82
(blonde man); Linographic p.64 (running); NASA Public Affairs Division p.52
(Man on moon/Kennedy Space Center); Oxford University Press pp.6 (number
3) 6 (number 2/Photodisc), 11 (Laszlo/Gareth Boden), 11 (Simon/Image
Source), 14 (man/Photodisc), 14 (woman/Photodisc), 23 (Belle/Fancy), 23
(James/Photodisc), 23 (boy/Image Source) 23 (girl/Blend Images) 23 (Carrie/
Photodisc), 24 (camera/CreativeAct - Technology series), 26 (man/Blend
Images), 31 (woman/David Jordan), 32 (orange/Photodisc), 32 (newspaper/
Brand X Pictures), 35 (girl doing homework/Corbis/Digital Stock), 35 (man on
couch/Image Source), 44 (boys shopping), 53 (Tom/Photodisc), 58 (tennis/
Creatas), 60 (friends around a table/Flying Colours Ltd./Digital Vision), 64
(baby walking/Photodisc), 64 (skier/Photodisc), 64 (playing guitar/Stockbyte),
64 (singing/RubberBall), 71 (post office/Gareth Boden), 71 (news agent/E.
Dygas/Digital Vision), 71 (cloths shopping/ColorBlind Images/Blend Images),
71 (buying fruit/Simon Potter/Image Source), 71 (man in restaurant/Nick
White/Image Source), 72 (lunch/Stockbyte), 74 (cooked breakfast/Stockbyte),
74 (scampi & chips/Photodisc), 74 (sandwich/Mark Mason), 74 (roast beef/
Photodisc), 77 (school class/Corel), 77 (man at cafe/Photodisc), 79 (barbecue/
image100), 82 (blonde girl/PhotoAlto), 82 (girl with glasses/Photodisc), 84
(raising hand in class/Corbis/Digital Stock), 84 (school/Photodisc), 84 (woman/
Gareth Boden), 86 (woman/Image Source), 87 (looking at map/Chris King);
Photolibrary Group pp.6 (terminal 1/Raimund Linke/Mauritius), 8 (waving/
Jupiterimages/Pixiand), 8 (female shopper/Simon Winnall/Britain on View),
11 (Hayley); Press Association Images pp.38 (Barack Obama/Deniz Arslan/AA/
ABACA), 52 (tanks), 52 (Berlin Wall/Thomas Kienzle/Associated Press), 54
(Andy Warhol/Associated Press), 54 (Princess Diana/Mark Lennihan/
Associated Press); Rex Features pp.25 (Queen Elizabeth II), 25 (Abramovich/
Sipa Press), 40 (Johnny Depp/Sipa Press); Shutterstock pp.6 (number 6), 6
(number 5/Matt Trommer), 6 (number 10/Emin Ozkan), 6 (number9/Drilea
Cristian), 17 (businessman/Yuri Arcurs), 24 (guitar/Elnur), 24 (CD cases/
Mariano N. Ruiz), 24 (motorbike/adsheyn), 24 (laptop/Terekhov Igor), 24
(bicycle/Aleks Key), 32 (ice cream cone/Fotocrisis), 32 (hamburger/ukrphoto),
32 (jeans), 64 (man in tie/BelleMedia), 64 (horse rider/cynoclub), 71 (shopping
for cosmetics/Diego Cervo), 77 (reading/Phase4Photography), 77 (working on
computer/Christopher Halloran), 77 (talking on phone/Brendan Howard), 79t
(Wedding/Michal Bednarek); Zooid Pictures p.32 (dictionary/Ned Coomes),

Commissioned photography by: Gareth Boden p.11 Rosely, p.18 Metro 5

Illustrations by: Gill Button pp.14, 19, 29 (ex 2), 42, 43, 48 (ex 8), 59, 65, 68, 71,
80; Mark Duffin pp.6 (crossword), 15, 16 (crossword), 28, 29 (ex 3), 71 (ex 5),
76; Kev Hopgood p.55; Ned Jolliffe pp.10, 11, 16, 49; Joe McLaren pp.7, 70;
Annabel Milne pp.34, 45, 46, 48 (ex 9), 61, 73; Gavin Reece pp.5, 8, 12, 20, 22,
23, 36, 47, 66, 72, 78, 83